CONSTITUTIONAL RIGHTS, MORAL CONTROVERSY, AND THE SUPREME COURT

In *Constitutional Rights, Moral Controversy, and the Supreme Court*, Michael J. Perry examines three of the most disputed constitutional issues of our time: capital punishment, state laws banning abortion, and state policies denying the benefit of law to same-sex unions.

Perry, a leading constitutional scholar, explains that if a majority of the justices of the Supreme Court believes that a law violates the Constitution, it does not necessarily follow that the Court should rule that the law is unconstitutional. In cases in which it is argued that a law violates the Constitution, the Supreme Court must decide which of two importantly different questions it should address: (1) Is the challenged law unconstitutional? (2) Is the lawmakers' judgment that the challenged law is *constitutional* a reasonable judgment? (One can answer both questions in the affirmative.)

By focusing on the death penalty, abortion, and same-sex unions, Perry provides new perspectives not only on moral controversies that implicate one or more constitutionally entrenched human rights, but also on the fundamental question of the Supreme Court's proper role in adjudicating such controversies.

Michael J. Perry holds a Robert W. Woodruff Chair at Emory University, where he teaches in the law school. Previously, he held the Howard J. Trienens Chair in Law at Northwestern University, where he taught for fifteen years, and the University Distinguished Chair in Law at Wake Forest University. Perry has written on American constitutional law and theory; law, morality, and religion; and human rights theory in more than sixty articles and ten books, most recently *Under God? Religious Faith and Liberal Democracy* (Cambridge, 2003) and *Toward a Theory of Human Rights: Religion, Law, Courts* (Cambridge, 2007).

Constitutional Rights, Moral Controversy, and the Supreme Court

MICHAEL J. PERRY

Emory University

CAMBRIDGE
UNIVERSITY PRESS

CAMBRIDGE UNIVERSITY PRESS
Cambridge, New York, Melbourne, Madrid, Cape Town, Singapore,
São Paulo, Delhi, Dubai, Tokyo, Mexico City

Cambridge University Press
32 Avenue of the Americas, New York, NY 10013-2473, USA

www.cambridge.org
Information on this title: www.cambridge.org/9780521184410

First published 2009
First paperback edition 2010

A catalog record for this publication is available from the British Library

Library of Congress Cataloging in Publication data

Perry, Michael J.
Constitutional rights, moral controversy, and the Supreme Court /
Michael J. Perry.
p. cm.
Includes bibliographical references and index.
ISBN 978-0-521-75595-5 (hardback)
1. Constitutional law – United States. 2. Civil rights – United States.
3. Political questions and judicial power – United States. 4. Capital
punishment – United States. 5. Same-sex marriage – United States.
6. Abortion – Law and legislation – United States. 7. Thayer, James Bradley,
1831–1902. I. Title.
KF8748.P39 2008
342.73–dc22 2008004208

ISBN 978-0-521-75595-5 Hardback
ISBN 978-0-521-18441-0 Paperback

For my colleagues at Emory University

Contents

Acknowledgments

I am grateful to my colleagues at Emory University – to whom I dedicate this book – for the opportunities they have given me over the past several years to present and discuss work that now appears, in revised (and, I hope, improved) form, in this book. I am also grateful to the Emory students who have taken my constitutional law courses; they have been, for me, thoughtful, challenging, and indispensable conversation partners.

I owe a special word of thanks to many people in numerous non-Emory venues for having invited me to present and discuss work that now appears in this book: University of Alabama School of Law (September 2005); King College, Bristol, Tennessee (October 2005); University of Dayton School of Law (February 2006); University of Georgia School of Law

(March 2006); Loyola University of Chicago School of Law (March 2006); Brooklyn Law School (April 2006); University of Texas School of Law (April 2006); American Philosophical Association, Central Division, Chicago, Illinois (April 2006); Congress of Constitutional Studies, São Paulo, Brazil (September 2006); American Philosophical Association, Eastern Division (December 2006); Marlboro College, Marlboro, Vermont (March 2007); University of Utah School of Law and Department of Philosophy (March 2007); Vanderbilt University Center for Ethics and School of Law (March 2007); Florida State University College of Law (April 2007); Cornell University School of Law (April 2007); College Theology Society, Dayton, Ohio (June 2007); and Walsh University, Canton, Ohio (March 2008).

I am indebted to my editor at Cambridge University Press, Andy Beck, for his continuing support and encouragement, and to Ronald Cohen, whose exemplary editorial work improved the manuscript in many ways.

Finally, I am grateful both to the readers who evaluated the manuscript for Cambridge University Press, for their extensive and helpful comments, and to Dan Ra and Dan Adams, for their work on the index.

Introduction: A (Partial) Theory of Judicial Review

> The first virtue of any theory of constitutional adjudication is a theory of judicial review – of judicial power to override legislative commands.[1]

The Constitution of the United States establishes the national government – or, as it is typically called, the federal government – and allocates power (1) among the three branches (legislative, executive, and judicial) of the national government, and (2) between the national government and the governments of the states. The Constitution also limits the power of government. Most of the Constitution's power-limiting provisions, such as the Eighth Amendment's ban on cruel and

[1] Adrian Vermeule, "Common Law Constitutionalism and the Limits of Reason," 107 Columbia L. Rev. 1482, 1532 (2007).

unusual punishments, articulate what we today call "human rights." I am concerned in this book with the proper role of the Supreme Court of the United States in enforcing the Constitution's power-limiting provisions – in enforcing, that is, the human rights articulated by those provisions. My animating concern, in short, is the Court's proper role in enforcing constitutionally entrenched human rights.

Consider the following twofold proposition, which is so uncontroversial as to be banal: That a law (or other government policy) is morally objectionable or otherwise woefully misguided does not mean that the law violates the Constitution; so, that a law is woefully misguided does not mean that the Supreme Court (or any other court) should rule that the law is unconstitutional. (As Supreme Court Justice Thurgood Marshall was fond of saying: "The Constitution does not prohibit legislatures from enacting stupid laws.")[2] Now, consider a second proposition, which *is* controversial, and which I defend in this book: That the Court (or a majority of it) believes that a law is unconstitutional – for example, a law authorizing the imposition of capital punishment – does not mean that the Court should rule that the law is unconstitutional.

[2] See David Stout, "Justices Back New York Trial Judge System," New York Times, January 16, 2008 (quoting Justice John Paul Stevens quoting his "esteemed former colleague, Thurgood Marshall").

Relatedly, that a citizen – even a citizen who is, *mirabile dictu*, a constitutional scholar! – believes that a law is unconstitutional does not mean that he should want the Court to rule that the law is unconstitutional. It is quite common for constitutional scholars, once they have argued that a law is unconstitutional, to conclude or imply that the Court should so rule (or that the Court was justified in so ruling) without realizing that they need a further argument to support the proposition that the Court should so rule.[3] However, whether a law is unconstitutional and whether the Supreme Court should so rule are distinct questions: The answer to each question may be affirmative, but that the answer to the former question is affirmative, as I explain in this book, does not entail that the answer to the latter question is affirmative.[4]

[3] For a prominent recent example of this phenomenon, see Jack M. Balkin, "Abortion and Original Meaning," 24 Constitutional Commentary (2007); available at http://ssrn.com/abstract=925558.

[4] In this book, I typically talk about the constitutionality of laws and other government policies. (A law necessarily represents a government policy.) But constitutional cases do not always seem to involve the constitutionality of a law or other government policy; constitutional cases sometimes involve the constitutionality of a government official's (for example, a policeman's) behavior. Nonetheless, such cases do involve – they necessarily (if implicitly) involve – the constitutionality of a government policy – namely, the policy of permitting the government official to engage in the behavior at issue. If a law or other government policy forbade the official to engage in the behavior at issue, the question of the constitutionality of the behavior would not need to be addressed; if, however, no government policy forbids the official to engage in the behavior, the constitutional question must be

This book is, in part, an essay in constitutional theory. In the United States, constitutional theory comprises two main questions:

1. What does it mean – or, at least, what *should* it mean – to "interpret" a constitutional provision? For example, how should one go about deciding what "cruel and unusual" means in the Eighth Amendment's ban on cruel and unusual punishments?
2. What is the proper role of the courts in enforcing a constitutional provision? More precisely, should the courts be deferential – or not – in enforcing a constitutional provision: Should the courts strike down a law claimed to violate a constitutional provision if they agree that the law violates the provision, or, instead, should they strike down the law only if they conclude that the counterclaim that the law does not violate the provision is unreasonable?

Although in the last thirty years or so constitutional scholars have devoted ample attention to the first question, they have largely neglected the second question. This book is in part an effort to correct that state of affairs.

addressed. And to rule on the constitutionality of the behavior is necessarily to rule on the constitutionality of government's permitting the official to engage in the behavior.

Not that I neglect the first question: My discussion of the constitutionality of capital punishment (Chapter 3), of state refusals to extend the benefit of law to same-sex unions (Chapter 4), and of state bans on pre-viabiality abortions (Chapter 5) presupposes an "originalist" answer to the first question, and I explain and defend that answer in Chapter 3. (Aren't we all – well, almost all – originalists now?[5] To be an originalist is not necessarily to believe that the judiciary should overturn every constitutional doctrine that cannot be justified on an originalist basis. Some such doctrines, after all, have achieved the status of what I have elsewhere called "constitutional bedrock": They are well-settled and there is no significant support – in particular, among the political elites – for abandoning the doctrines.)[6] But this book is mainly about – I spend most of my time in this book addressing – the second question, and *what I say in this book in response to the second question does not depend on what I say in response to the first*. In responding to the second question, I elaborate, defend, and illustrate (what I call) the Thayerian approach to constitutional

[5] See Chapter 3, n. 2.

[6] See Michael J. Perry, We the People: The Fourteenth Amendment and the Supreme Court 19–23 (1999). "Making room for stare decisis in the practice of originalism does not make one unprincipled or inconsistent; it merely reflects a normatively grounded theory of constitutional interpretation." Kurt T. Lash, "Originalism, Popular Sovereignty, and *Reverse* Stare Decisis," 93 Virginia L. Rev. 1437, 1481 (2007). (Lash's important article is well worth reading.)

adjudication. The question whether one should accept the originalist approach – or, at least, *an* originalist approach – to constitutional interpretation and the question whether one should accept the Thayerian approach to constitutional adjudication are entirely distinct questions; an affirmative answer to the former question does not entail an affirmative answer to the latter, nor does a negative answer to the former question entail a negative answer to the latter. Again, I am mainly concerned in this book with the latter question.

Caveat emptor. One of my principal concerns in this book is how, given what the Constitution means, the Supreme Court should resolve certain constitutional controversies. So, in the chapters that follow – in particular, the chapters in which I address the constitutional controversies concerning capital punishment, same-sex unions, and abortion – I am interested in what the Constitution means, not in what the Supreme Court says it means. There are more than enough materials in the marketplace for readers who want to know what the Court says the Constitution means, and more than enough materials, too, for readers looking for commentary on how, given what the Court says the Constitution means – given, that is, existing constitutional doctrine, some of which is quite misguided – the Court should resolve one or another constitutional controversy.

Introduction: A (Partial) Theory of Judicial Review

In this book, I continue to pursue an inquiry I began in the final part of my previous book, *Toward a Theory of Human Rights* (2007). The approach to constitutional adjudication – the theory of judicial review – I defend in this, my tenth book, is different, to say the least, from the approach I defended in my first book, *The Constitution, the Courts, and Human Rights* (1982), which was published over a quarter century ago. "Only the hand that erases can write the true thing," said Meister Eckhart.

CHAPTER ONE

Human Rights: From Morality to Constitutional Law

My aim in this chapter is to provide some conceptual and normative background and context for the rest of the book. I do so by addressing three questions: What is the morality of human rights; that is, what is the morality that grounds the law of human rights? How does the morality of human rights ground the law of human rights? Why do most liberal democracies – including the United States – entrench some human rights laws in their constitutions?

I. The morality of human rights

Although the morality of human rights is only one morality among many, it has become the dominant morality of our time; indeed, unlike any morality before it, the morality of human rights has become a truly global morality.[1] (Relatedly, the language of human rights has become the moral *lingua franca*.)[2] Nonetheless, the morality of human rights is not well understood. What does the morality of human rights hold?

The International Bill of Rights, as it is informally known, consists of three documents: the Universal Declaration of Human Rights, the International Covenant on Civil and Political Rights, and the International Covenant on Economic, Social, and Cultural Rights.[3] The Universal Declaration refers,

[1] This is not to say that the morality of human rights is new; in one or another version, it is a very old morality. See Leszek Kolakowski, Modernity on Endless Trial 214 (1990) (explaining that "the notion of the immutable rights of individuals goes back to the Christian belief in the autonomous status and irreplaceable value of the human personality"). Nonetheless, the emergence of the morality of human rights in international law, in the period since the end of World War II, is a profoundly important development: "Until World War II, most legal scholars and governments affirmed the general proposition, albeit not in so many words, that international law did not impede the natural right of each equal sovereign to be monstrous to his or her subjects." Tom J. Farer & Felice Gaer, "The UN and Human Rights: At the End of the Beginning," in Adam Roberts & Benedict Kingsbury, eds., United Nations, Divided World 240 (2d ed. 1993).

[2] See Jürgen Habermas, Religion and Rationality: Essays on Reason, God, and Modernity 153–54 (Eduardo Mendieta, ed., 2002): "Notwithstanding their European origins, ... [i]n Asia, Africa, and South America, [human rights now] constitute the only language in which the opponents and victims of murderous regimes and civil wars can raise their voices against violence, repression, and persecution, against injuries to their human dignity."

[3] The Universal Declaration was adopted and proclaimed by the General Assembly of the United Nations on December 10, 1948. The International Covenant on Civil and Political Rights (ICCPR) and the International Covenant on Economic, Social, and Cultural Rights (ICESCR), which are treaties and as such are binding on the several state parties thereto, were meant, in part, to elaborate the various rights specified

in its preamble, to "the inherent dignity ... of all members of the human family" and states, in Article 1, that "[a]ll members of the human family are born free and equal in dignity and rights ... and should act towards one another in a spirit of brotherhood." The two covenants each refer, in their preambles, to "the inherent dignity ... of all members of the human family" and to "the inherent dignity of the human person" – from which, the covenants insist, "the equal and inalienable rights of all members of the human family ... derive."[4]

in the Universal Declaration. The ICCPR and the ICESCR were each adopted and opened for signature, ratification, and accession by the General Assembly of the United Nations on December 16, 1966. The ICESCR entered into force on January 3, 1976, and as of June 2004 had 149 state parties. The ICCPR entered into force on March 23, 1976, and as of June 2004 had 152 state parties. The United States is a party to the ICCPR but not to the ICESCR. In October 1977, President Jimmy Carter signed both the ICCPR and the ICESCR. Although the United States Senate has not ratified the ICESCR, the Senate in September 1992, with the support of President George H. W. Bush, ratified the ICCPR (subject to certain "reservations, understandings and declarations" that are not relevant here; see 138 Cong. Rec. S 4781–84 (daily ed. April 2, 1992)).

[4] The relevant wording of the two preambles is as follows:

> The State Parties to the present Covenant,
>
> Considering that ... recognition of the inherent dignity and of the equal and inalienable rights of all members of the human family is the foundation of freedom, justice, and peace in the world.
>
> Recognizing that these rights derive from the inherent dignity of the human person. ...
>
> Agree upon the following articles: ...

According to the International Bill of Rights, then, and also according to the constitutions of many liberal democracies,[5] the morality of human rights – the morality that grounds the law of human rights – consists of a twofold claim, the first part of which is that *each and every human being has equal inherent dignity*.[6]

- *The Oxford English Dictionary* gives the following principal definition of "dignity": "The quality of being worthy or honourable; worthiness, worth, nobleness, excellence."[7]
- To say that every human being has "inherent" dignity is to say that the fundamental dignity every human being possesses, he or she possesses *not* as a member of one or

[5] See David Kretzmer & Eckart Klein, eds., The Concept of Human Dignity in Human Rights Discourse, v–vi, 41–42 (2002); Mirko Bagaric & James Allan, "The Vacuous Concept of Dignity," 5 J. Human Rights 257, 261–63 (2006). See also Vicki C. Jackson, "Constitutional Dialogue and Human Dignity: States and Transnational Constitutional Discourse," 65 Montana L. Rev. 15 (2004).

[6] As a descriptive matter, the morality of human rights holds not that every human being has inherent dignity, but only that every *born* human being has inherent dignity. See Michael J. Perry, Toward a Theory of Human Rights: Religion, Law, Courts 54 (2007). Except when discussing abortion, as I do in Chapter 4 of the present book, I generally bracket the born/unborn distinction and say simply that according to the morality of human rights, every human being has inherent dignity. I argue elsewhere that we who affirm that every born human being has inherent dignity have good reason to affirm as well that every unborn human being has inherent dignity. See id. at 54–59.

[7] *Oxford English Dictionary* (2d ed. 1991). Cf. Christopher McCrudden, "Human Dignity," Oxford Legal Studies Research Paper Series No. 10/2006, available at http://papers.ssrn.com/abstract=899687.

another group (racial, ethnic, national, religious, and so on), *not* as a man or a woman, *not* as someone who has done or achieved something, and so on, *but simply as a human being*.[8]

- To say that every human being has "equal" inherent dignity is to say that having inherent dignity is not a condition that admits of degrees: Just as no pregnant woman can be more – or less – pregnant than another pregnant woman, no human being can have more – or less – inherent dignity than another human being. According to the morality of human rights, "[a]ll members of the human family are born . . . equal in dignity . . ." Hereafter, when I say "inherent dignity," I mean "equal inherent dignity."[9]

[8] The ICCPR, in Article 26, bans "discrimination on any ground such as race, colour, sex, language, religion, political or other opinion, national or social origin, property, birth or other status." See Peter Berger, "On the Obsolescence of the Concept of Honor," in Stanley Hauerwas & Alasdair MacIntyre, eds., Revisions: Changing Perspectives in Moral Philosophy 172, 176 (1983): "Dignity . . . always relates to the intrinsic humanity divested of all socially imposed roles or norms. It pertains to the self as such, to the individual regardless of his position in society. This becomes very clear in the classic formulations of human rights, from the Preamble to the Declaration of Independence to the Universal Declaration of Human Rights of the United Nations." Cf. Charles E. Curran, "Catholic Social Teaching: A Historical and Ethical Analysis 1891-Present 132 (2002): "Human dignity comes from God's free gift; it does not depend on human effort, work, or accomplishments. All human beings have a fundamental, equal dignity because all share the generous gift of creation and redemption from God. . . . Consequently, all human beings have the same fundamental dignity, whether they are brown, black, red, or white; rich or poor, young or old; male or female; healthy or sick."

[9] For a skeptical account of talk about inherent dignity, see Bagaric & Allan, n. 5. "Dignity is a vacuous concept." Id. at 269.

The second part of the claim is that *the inherent dignity of human beings has a normative force for us, in this sense: We should live our lives in accord with the fact that every human being has inherent dignity; that is, we should respect – we have conclusive reason to respect – the inherent dignity of every human being.*[10]

There is another way to state the twofold claim that is the morality of human rights: Every human being has inherent dignity and is *"inviolable"*: not-to-be-violated.[11] According to the morality of human rights, one can violate a human being either explicitly or implicitly. One violates a human being *explicitly* if one explicitly denies that she (or he) has inherent dignity. (The Nazis, for example, explicitly denied that the Jews had inherent dignity.)[12] One violates a human being *implicitly* if one treats her as if she lacks inherent dignity, either by doing do to her what one would not do to her, or

[10] I say that the morality of human rights consists of a *twofold* claim, rather than that it consists of two claims, as a way of emphasizing that according to the morality of human rights, the claim that every human being has inherent dignity is not an independent claim but is inextricably connected to the further claim that we should live our lives in a way that respects the inherent dignity of every human being.

[11] *The Oxford English Dictionary* gives the following principal definition of "inviolable": "not to be violated; not liable or allowed to suffer violence; to be kept sacredly free from profanation, infraction, or assault." *Oxford English Dictionary* (2d ed. 1991).

[12] See Michael Burleigh & Wolfgang Wipperman, The Racial State: Germany, 1933–1945 (1991); Johannes Morsink, "World War Two and the Universal Declaration," 15 Human Rights Q. 357, 363 (1993); Claudia Koonz, The Nazi Conscience (2003).

by refusing to do for her what one would not refuse to do for her, if one genuinely perceived her to have inherent dignity. (Even if the Nazis had not explicitly denied that the Jews had inherent dignity, they would have implicitly denied it: The Nazis did to the Jews what no one who genuinely perceived the Jews to have inherent dignity would have done to them.) In the context of the morality of human rights, to say (1) that every human being has inherent dignity, and we should live our lives accordingly (that is, in a way that respects that dignity), is to say (2) that every human being has inherent dignity and is inviolable: not-to-be-violated, in the sense of "violate" just indicated. To affirm the morality of human rights is to affirm the twofold claim that every human being has inherent dignity and is inviolable.

If it is true, *why* is it true – *in virtue of what* is it true – that every human being has inherent dignity and is inviolable?[13] That the International Bill of Rights is (famously) silent on that question is not surprising, given the plurality of religious and non-religious views that existed among those who bequeathed us the Universal Declaration and the two

[13] Cf. Jeff McMahan, "When Not to Kill or Be Killed," Times Lit. Supp., August 7, 1998, at 31 (reviewing Frances Myrna Kamm, Morality, Mortality (Vol. II): Rights, Duties, and Status (1997)): "Understanding the basis of our alleged inviolability is crucial both for determining whether it is plausible to regard ourselves as inviolable, and for fixing the boundaries of the class of inviolable beings."

covenants.[14] Indeed, the claim that every human being has inherent dignity and is inviolable is deeply problematic for many secular thinkers, because the claim is difficult – perhaps to the point of impossible – to align with one of their fundamental convictions, which Bernard Williams called "Nietzsche's thought": "[T]here is, not only no God, but no metaphysical order of any kind..."[15] I have explained elsewhere why I am skeptical that there is a plausible secular ground for the morality of human rights,[16] but be that as it may, the

[14] See Jacques Maritain, "Introduction," in UNESCO, Human Rights: Comments and Interpretation 9–17 (1949). Maritain wrote: "[W]e agree about the rights but on condition that no one asks us why." Id. at 9. (See also Youngjae Lee, "International Consensus as Persuasive Authority in the Eighth Amendment," http://ssrn.com/abstract=959706 (2007): "International human rights treaties are... willfully silent about the reasons behind the norms that they adopt.") However, Maritain was wrong: There was agreement *both* about "the rights" (actually, about *some* rights) *and* about a part of the "why": namely, that every human being has inherent dignity. Again, the Declaration explicitly refers, in its preamble, to "the inherent dignity... of all members of the human family" and states, in Article 1, that "[a]ll members of the human family are born free and equal in dignity and rights... and should act towards one another in a spirit of brotherhood." So what Maritain should have said was this: "We agree about the rights. We even agree about the inherent dignity – but on condition that no one asks us *why* every human being has inherent dignity."

[15] Bernard Williams, "Republican and Galilean," New York Rev., November 8, 1990, at 45, 48 (reviewing Charles Taylor, Sources of the Self: The Making of Modern Identity (1989)). See Perry, Toward a Theory of Human Rights, n. 6, at 14–29. Cf. John M. Rist, Real Ethics: Rethinking the Foundations of Morality 2 (2002): "[Plato] came to believe that if morality, as more than 'enlightened' self-interest, is to be rationally justifiable, it must be established on metaphysical foundations..."

[16] See Michael J. Perry, "Morality and Normativity," 13 Legal Theory 211 (2008). See also Perry, Toward a Theory of Human Rights, n. 6, at 1–29. According to Jürgen Habermas:

morality of human rights – the morality that grounds the law of human rights – is, without question, the dominant morality of our time.

II. From morality to law

By the morality of human rights, I mean the morality that grounds – that is a principal ground of – the law of human rights.[17] How, precisely, does the morality of human rights ground the law of human rights?

> Christianity has functioned for the normative self-understanding of modernity as more than a mere precursor or a catalyst. Egalitarian universalism, from which sprang the ideas of freedom and social solidarity, of an autonomous conduct of life and emancipation, of the individual morality of conscience, human rights, and democracy. is the direct heir to the Judaic ethic of justice and the Christian ethic of love. This legacy, substantially unchanged, has been the object of continual critical appropriation and reinterpretation. To this day, there is no alternative to it. And in light of the current challenges of the postnational constellation, we continue to draw on the substance of this heritage. Everything else is just idle postmodern talk.

Jürgen Habermas, Time of Transitions 150–51 (2006).

I concur in Brian Schaefer's judgment that "foundationless" approaches to human rights are deeply problematic. See Brian Schaefer, "Human Rights: Problems with the Foundationless Approach," 31 Soc. Theory & Practice 27 (2005) (critiquing the putatively foundationless approaches of Michael Ignatieff and Richard Rorty). See also Serena Parekh, "Resisting 'Full and Torpid' Assent: Returning to the Debate Over the Foundations of Human Rights," 29 Human Rights Q. 754 (2007).

17 The morality of human rights – the proposition that every human being has inherent dignity and is inviolable – is not the only ground of the law of human rights. See Perry, Toward a Theory of Human Rights, n. 6, at 25–26. But it is, as I explained in the preceding section

Again, the morality of human rights holds that every human being has inherent dignity and is "inviolable": not-to-be-violated. So we who affirm the morality of human rights, *because* we affirm it, should do what we can, all things considered – we have conclusive reason to do what we can, all things considered – to prevent human beings, including government officials, from doing things that violate human beings either explicitly or implicitly.[18] (The "doing" may be a not-doing,

of this chapter, the principal ground articulated by the international law of human rights.

[18] The "all things considered" will be, in many contexts, indeterminate. What Amartya Sen, borrowing from Immanuel Kant, calls the distinction between "perfect" and "imperfect" duties is relevant here – though I would mark the distinction with different terms: "determinate" and "indeterminate" duties. As Sen remarks, "[t]he perfectly specified demand not to torture anyone is supplemented by the more general, and less easily specified, requirement to consider the ways and means through which torture can be prevented and then to decide what one should, thus, reasonably do." Amartya Sen, "Elements of a Theory of Human Rights," 32 Philosophy & Public Affairs 315, 322 (2004). Sen elaborates:

> Even though recognition of human rights (with their associated claims and obligations) are ethical affirmations, they need not, by themselves, deliver a complete blueprint for evaluative assessment. An agreement of human rights does involve a firm commitment, to wit, to give reasonable consideration to the duties that follow from that ethical endorsement. But even with agreement on these affirmations, there can still be serious debates, particularly in the case of imperfect obligations, on (i) the ways in which the attention that is owed to human rights should be best paid, (ii) how the different types of human rights should be weighed against each other and their respective demands integrated together, (iii) how the claims of human rights should be consolidated with other evaluative concerns that may also deserve ethical attention, and so on. A theory of human rights can leave room for further discussions, disputations and arguments. The approach of open public

a refusal to help.) Moreover, we who affirm the morality of human rights, *because* we affirm it, have conclusive reason to do what we can, all things considered, to *do more than* prevent human beings from doing things that violate human beings: We also have conclusive reason to do what we can, all things considered, to prevent human beings from doing things that, even if they do not violate human beings, even implicitly, nonetheless cause them unwarranted suffering (or other harm). I am referring here to serious, not trivial, human suffering. In Germany during World War II, Dietrich Bonhoeffer observed that "[w]e have for once learned to see the great events of world history from below, from the perspective of the outcast, the suspects, the maltreated, the powerless, the oppressed, the reviled – in short, from the perspective of those who suffer."[19] If we refuse to do what we can (all things considered) to prevent human beings from violating human beings or otherwise causing them unwarranted suffering –

> reasoning...can definitively settle some disputes about coverage and content (including the identification of some clearly sustainable rights and others that would be hard to sustain), but may have to leave others, at least tentatively, unsettled. The admissibility of a domain of continued dispute is no embarrassment to a theory of human rights.

Id. at 322–23.

19 Dietrich Bonhoeffer, "After Ten Years: A Letter to the Family and Conspirators," in Dietrich Bonhoeffer, A Testament to Freedom 482, 486 (Geoffrey B. Kelly & F. Burton Nelson, eds.; rev. ed. HarperSanFrancisco 1995). "After Ten Years" bears the date "Christmas 1942."

and by "we" I mean here primarily the collective we, as in "We the People," acting through our elected representatives – we refuse to do what we can to protect the victims *and thereby violate them*: We treat them – "those who suffer" – as if they lack inherent dignity by refusing to do for them what no one would refuse to do for them who genuinely perceived them to have inherent dignity. Primo Levi wrote that "if we see the severe torment that pain is causing, and do nothing, then we ourselves are the Tormenter."[20] In the same spirit, Martin Luther King Jr. declared that "[m]an's inhumanity to man is not only perpetrated by the vitriolic actions of those who are bad. It is also perpetrated by the vitiating inaction of those who are good."[21] Sometimes we violate a human being not by doing something to hurt her but by refusing to do something to protect her. "Sins against human rights are not only those of commission, but those of omission as well."[22]

To say, in the present context, that an instance of human suffering is "unwarranted" is to say that the act that causes the suffering – even if the act is a refusal to act, a refusal to intervene to diminish the suffering – is not warranted, that it is not justified. Not justified *from whose perspective*? It is scarcely

[20] I have not been able to locate the source of this statement.
[21] Quoted in Nicholas D. Kristof, "The American Witness," New York Times, March 2, 2005.
[22] Charles L. Black Jr., A New Birth of Freedom: Human Rights, Named and Unnamed 133 (1999).

surprising that the act, and therefore the suffering it causes, may be justified from the perspective of those whose act is in question. But theirs is not the relevant perspective. The relevant perspective belongs to those of us who, in coming face to face with the suffering, must decide what, if anything, to do, or to try to do, about it; in making that decision, we must reach our own judgment about whether the suffering is warranted.

We can now see how the morality of human rights grounds the law of human rights; we can now see, that is, how a commitment to the morality of human rights – to the inherent dignity and inviolability of every human being – grounds a commitment to legislating certain rights – more precisely, to legislating certain rights-claims: We who affirm the morality of human rights, *because* we affirm it, should press our elected representatives not to do anything that would violate human beings or otherwise cause them unwarranted suffering, *but we should also press them to legislate certain rights-claims: claims about what may not be done to, or about what must be done for, human beings*. As we have learned in the period since the end of World War II, the law of human rights is an important way of trying to prevent government officials – and others[23] –

[23] See Henry J. Steiner, "Human Rights: The Deepening Footprint," 20 Harvard Human Rights Journal 7, 9 (2007):

> Increasingly, international norms and institutions are reaching beyond the state to regulate large categories of non-state actors, from political associations and business corporations to ordinary

from violating human beings or otherwise causing them unwarranted suffering.

This seems the appropriate point at which to emphasize that "human *right*" is short for "human *rights-claim*": a claim, grounded on the inherent dignity and inviolability of every human being, about what may not be done to, or about what must be done for, human beings. A human rights-claim is typically either a legal claim or a moral claim: legal, if the claim is about what the law forbids or requires;[24] moral, if the claim is about what morality forbids or requires.[25] Human

individuals. They do so directly under international law, through treaty norms defining personal international crimes like crimes against humanity that cover state and non-state actors. They also do so indirectly, and far more broadly, by requiring state parties to protect their population against rights-violating conduct of non-state actors, often through treaties that specify what non-state activity – such as discriminatory corporate employment, or family violence – the state must proscribe and act against. Whatever its accuracy at the movement's foundation, the notion that the human rights movement regulates only state conduct is at best an historical observation. As it develops, human rights law continues to erode the long-standing notion of a public–private divide, in the sense of state and non-state actors, where only the former is subject to regulation under international law.

24 A legal claim that A may not do X to B is a legal rights-claim, because that A has a legal *duty* (obligation) not to do X to B entails that B has a legal *right* that A not do X to him; similarly, a legal claim that A must do Y for B is a legal rights-claim, because that A has a legal *duty* to do Y for B entails that B has a legal *right* that A do Y for him.

25 I have confessed elsewhere to my discomfort with articulating moral claims in terms of "rights." See Perry, Toward a Theory of Human Rights, n. 6, at xii–xiii.

rights-claims, both legal and moral, are often universal, in the sense that they specify what those subject to the right may not do to *any* human being or what they must do for *every* human being. But human rights-claims are not always universal; for example, a human rights-claim, whether legal or moral, may specify what may not be done to, or what must be done for, just some human beings – children, for example, or impoverished human beings living in an affluent society.

III. Why liberal democracies entrench certain human rights laws

Not every country that advertises itself as a democracy is in fact a democracy.[26] (The official name of East Germany, translated into English, was the German Democratic Republic;

[26] For a "modest" – and woefully incomplete – definition of democracy, see Andrew Koppelman, "Talking to the Boss: On Robert Bennett and the Counter-Majoritarian Difficulty," 95 Northwestern U.L. Rev. 955, 956–57 (2001):

> [Joseph] Shumpeter . . . proposes the following, more modest definition of democracy: "the democratic method is that institutional arrangement for arriving at political decisions in which individuals acquire the power to decide by means of a competitive struggle for the people's vote." The people influence political decisions by voting in elections and "do not control their political leaders in any way except by refusing to reelect them or the parliamentary majorities that support them."
>
> The politician is vulnerable to losing his office unless he continuously manages to attract votes. This creates an incentive for

the official name of North Korea, translated, is the Democratic People's Republic of Korea.)[27] There is a difference between a true (authentic, genuine) democracy – that is, a liberal democracy – and a *faux* democracy.[28] What is a "liberal"

> him to pay attention to what voters want. And this incentive guarantees that, in a democracy, the government will not act in a way that attracts the wrath of an electoral majority – or, if it does, that it won't keep it up for long.

(Quoting Joseph A. Shumpeter, Capitalism, Socialism, and Democracy (3d ed. 1950).) According to Koppelman, "[Joseph] Shumpeter is entirely free of . . . mushy sentimentalism about majoritarianism . . ." Id. at 956. See also Richard A. Posner, "Enlightened Despot," New Republic, April 23, 2007, at 53, 54: "Political democracy in the modern sense means a system of government in which the key officials stand for election at relatively short intervals and thus are accountable to the citizenry."

For a fuller and much more satisfactory account of democracy, see Kenneth Roth, "Despots Masquerading as Democrats," in Human Rights Watch, World Report 2008 1, 5–6 (2008); Larry Diamond, The Spirit of Democracy 20–26 (2008).

27 See Roth, n. 26, at 7: "As the Burmese junta rounded up protesting monks and violently suppressed dissent, it spoke of the need for 'disciplined democracy.' China has long promoted 'socialist democracy,' by which it means a top-down centrism that eliminates minority views."

28 Or, as one scholar of democracy has recently called it, "pseudodemocracy." Diamond, n. 26, at 23. See Associated Press, "Report Says Democracies Enable Despots," New York Times, January 31, 2008:

> Authoritarian rulers are violating human rights around the world and getting away with it largely because the U.S., European and other established democracies accept their claims that holding elections makes them democratic, Human Rights Watch said in its annual report [today].
>
> By failing to demand that offenders honor their citizens' civil and political rights and other requirements of true democracy, Western democracies risk undermining human rights everywhere, the international rights watchdog said.
>
> Still, Kenneth Roth, Human Rights Watch's executive director, wrote in a segment of the report called "Despots Masquerading

democracy? Not everyone will give precisely the same answer, but according to a common – and attractive – account, which I accept, a "liberal" democracy is a democracy committed, first, to the proposition that each and every human being has inherent dignity and is inviolable and, second, to certain human rights.[29] A democracy is committed to the proposition

as Democrats": "It is a sign of hope that even dictators have come to believe that the route to legitimacy runs by way of democratic credentials."

[29] For example, philosopher Thomas Nagel has written that "[t]he term 'liberalism' applies to a wide range of political positions... But all liberal theories have this in common: they hold that the sovereign power of the state over the individual is bounded by a requirement that individuals remain inviolable in certain respects... The state... is subject to moral constraints that limit the subordination of the individual to the collective will and the collective interest." Thomas Nagel, "Progressive but Not Liberal," New York Review of Books, May 25, 2006. Similarly, philosopher Charles Larmore has argued that "our commitment to [liberal] democracy... cannot be understood except by appeal to a higher moral authority, which is the obligation to respect one another as persons." Charles Larmore, "The Moral Basis of Political Liberalism," 96 J. Philosophy 599, 624–25 (1999). Cf. Samuel Brittan, "Making Common Cause: How Liberals Differ, and What They Ought To Agree On," Times Literary Supplement, September 20, 1996, at 3, 4:

> [P]erhaps the litmus test of whether the reader is in any sense a liberal or not is Gladstone's foreign-policy speeches. In [one such speech,] taken from the late 1870s, around the time of the Midlothian campaign, [Gladstone] reminded his listeners that "the sanctity of life in the hill villages of Afghanistan among the winter snows, is as inviolable in the eye of almighty God as can be your own... that the law of mutual love is not limited by the shores of this island, is not limited by the boundaries of Christian civilization; that it passes over the whole surface of the earth, and embraces the meanest along with the greatest in its unmeasured scope." By all means smile at the oratory. But anyone who sneers at the underlying message is not a liberal in any sense of that word worth preserving.

that every human being has inherent dignity and is inviolable if in the political culture of the democracy the proposition is axiomatic; a democracy is committed to certain human rights if in the legal system of the democracy the rights are recognized and protected as fundamental legal rights. (The two commitments are connected: As I explained in the preceding section of this chapter, commitment to the proposition that every human being has inherent dignity and is inviolable is a principal reason for – a principal ground of – commitment to the law of human rights.) As it happens, most liberal democracies, including the United States, recognize and protect, as *fundamental* legal rights, the "certain human rights" to which they are committed by entrenching the rights in their constitutions.[30]

Listen, too, to Herman Melville: "But this august dignity I treat, of, is not the dignity of kings and robes, but that abounding dignity that has no robed investiture. Thou shalt see it shining in the arm that wields a pick or drives a spike; that democratic dignity which, on all hands, radiates without end from God Himself! The great God absolute! The centre and circumference of all democracy! His omnipresence, our divine equality!" Herman Melville, Moby Dick 126 (Penguin Classics ed. 1992).

30 What are the human rights to which *liberal* democracy, as such, is committed? Put another way: What are the human rights – the human rights-claims – that a democracy recognizes as fundamental legal rights-claims if the democracy is truly a *liberal* democracy? The interested reader will find the principal liberal-democratic rights (and other rights) set forth in the Universal Declaration of Human Rights and, more elaborately, in the International Covenant on Civil and Political Rights. For a succinct list of such rights, see Diamond, 26, at 22.

In most liberal democracies, some human rights laws are both (1) superior (lexically prior) to ordinary laws and (2) entrenched: *exceedingly difficult, sometimes to the point of practically impossible, to amend or repeal.* A conspicuous example of such a law is the Constitution of the United States, which by its own terms can be amended only by a complex, supermajoritarian political act:

> In the [United States, a constitutional] amendment is permitted only upon completion of supermajority requirements both in Congress and in the states: an amendment must be proposed, either by 2/3 of each House of Congress or by a convention called at the request of the legislatures of 2/3 of the states, and then the proposed amendment must be approved by the legislatures of or conventions in 3/4 of the states. This makes the U.S. Constitution one of the most deeply entrenched [in the world].[31]

It is precisely because it is so difficult to amend or repeal an entrenched law that entrenching certain human rights makes sense. As a commentator on the transition to democracy in South Africa observed, an entrenched "bill of rights was crucial . . . to the whole question of legitimacy of a post-apartheid regime. For its powerful symbolism would establish an arena not just for law, *but would also be a definition of what*

[31] Vicki C. Jackson & Mark Tushnet, Comparative Constitutional Law 414 (1999).

is, and is not, legitimate in politics."[32] This is not to deny that in liberal democracies, human rights that are not entrenched also have an important role to play in protecting human dignity and inviolability. In the United States, for example, many important human rights laws – the Civil Rights Act of 1964,[33] to name just one – are not entrenched. But most liberal democracies, including the United States, understandably entrench – by constitutionalizing – some human rights.

The United States Constitution consists mainly of two kinds of provisions:

(1) power-allocating provisions: (a) provisions that establish the national government – or, as it is typically called, the federal government – and allocate power (authority) among the three branches – the legislative, executive, and judicial branches – of the national government; and (b) provisions that allocate power between the national government and the governments of the states; and

(2) power-limiting provisions: provisions that limit the power of government.

[32] Martin Chanock, "A Post-Calvinist Catechism or a Post-Communist Manifesto? Intersecting Narratives in the South Africa Bill of Rights Debate," in Philip Alston, ed., Promoting Human Rights Through Bills of Rights: Comparative Perspectives 392, 394 (1999) (emphasis added).

[33] The Civil Rights Act of 1964, P.L. 88–352, was enacted, inter alia, "[t]o enforce the constitutional right to vote..."

Most of the power-limiting provisions, such as the Eighth Amendment's ban on cruel and unusual punishments,[34] articulate what we today recognize as human rights. So although it is more than a charter of human rights, the Constitution is a charter of human rights. Indeed, the Constitution, which is the earliest national charter of human rights in modern history, has been an inspiration for many later such charters,[35] including, in the last generation, the Charter of Rights and Freedoms of the Canadian Constitution (1982)[36] and the Bill of Rights of the South African Constitution (1996).[37]

[34] The Eighth Amendment states: "Excessive bail shall not be required, nor excessive fines imposed, nor cruel and unusual punishments inflicted."

[35] See William J. Brennan Jr., "The Worldwide Influence of the United States Constitution as a Charter of Human Rights," 15 Nova L. Rev. 1 (1991).

[36] The Canadian Charter of Rights and Freedoms is Part 1 of Canada's Constitution Act of 1982.

[37] The Bill of Rights is Chapter 2 of the Constitution of the Republic of South Africa (1996). See Christina Murray, "A Constitutional Beginning: Making South Africa's Final Constitution," 23 U. Arkansas at Little Rock L. Rev. 809 (2001); Chanock, n. 29. In her essay, Murray reports these interesting details:

> In March 1997, about seven million copies of the new constitution in pocket book size were distributed in South Africa. Four million went to high schools, two million were made available at post offices and another million were distributed to the police, army, prisons, and through civil organizations. These copies of the constitution were available in all eleven official languages and were accompanied by an illustrated guide, *You and the Constitution*, which, in thirty cheerfully illustrated pages, provided an introduction to the constitution.

Murray, supra, at 837.

The United States Constitution is silent about the fundamental moral ground of the human rights it entrenches. For that, we must look elsewhere – first and foremost to the Declaration of Independence, which affirms "that all men are created equal, that they are endowed by their Creator with certain unalienable Rights, that among these are Life, Liberty, and the pursuit of Happiness..." Those famous words, written in 1776, anticipate the twofold claim that is the morality of human rights: Every human being has inherent dignity and is inviolable. Charles Black contended for "the appropriateness of the Declaration as a *basis* for law, as a *nourisher* of law, whether or not it be taken to be law of its own unaided force."[38]

Addendum: What human rights does the United States Constitution entrench?

What human rights does the United States Constitution entrench? More precisely, what human rights have "We the People of the United States," who, in the words of the Preamble to the Constitution, "do ordain and establish this Constitution for the United States of America," constitutionalized and thereby entrenched?

[38] Black, A New Birth of Freedom, n. 22, at 8.

The original Constitution – the Constitution that was drafted in 1787 and entered into force in 1789 – contains only three legal claims that fit the relevant profile: claims about what government may not do or about what it must do, aimed at preventing goverment from violating human beings or otherwise causing them unwarranted suffering. Article I, Section 9, which is directed to Congress, states:

> The Privilege of the Writ of Habeas Corpus shall not be suspended unless when in Cases of Rebellion or Invasion the public safety may require it.
>
> No Bill of Attainder or ex post facto Law shall be passed.

Article III, Section 3 states:

> The Congress shall have the Power to declare the Punishment of Treason, but no Attainder of Treason shall work Corruption of Blood, or Forfeiture except during the Life of the Person attainted.

It is mainly in the Bill of Rights (1791) and the other amendments to the original Constitution that we find legal claims that fit the relevant profile.[39] The Bill of Rights consists

[39] However, not all the rights (rights-claims) in the Bill of Rights fit the relevant profile; not all Bill of Rights rights are human rights in the modern sense. For example, the Bill of Rights provides, in the Seventh Amendment, that "[i]n suits at common law, where the value in controversy shall exceed twenty dollars, the right of trial by jury shall be preserved..." Few if any of us today would argue that the right to have a jury rather than a judge decide one's civil case where the amount in controversy exceeds twenty dollars – or even twenty million dollars – is a human right.

of the first ten amendments to the Constitution.[40] Although the Bill of Rights was directed only to the federal government, not to the governments of the states, it is now constitutional bedrock that the Fourteenth Amendment (1868) makes the most important provisions of the Bill of Rights applicable to the states.[41] So it is not just the federal government but state governments too that may not, inter alia, prohibit the free exercise of religion, abridge the freedom of speech, or inflict cruel and unusual punishments.[42]

[40] However, the Tenth Amendment – which states that "[t]he powers not delegated to the United States by the Constitution, nor prohibited by it to the states, are reserved to the states respectively, or to the people" – is about the allocation of power between the national government and the governments of the states.

Like some other constitutional scholars, Daniel Farber reads the Ninth Amendment – which states that "[t]he enumeration in the Constitution, of certain rights, shall not be construed to deny or disparage others retained by the people" – to protect certain human rights. See Daniel A. Farber, Retained by the People: The "Silent" Ninth Amendment and the Constitutional Rights Americans Don't Know They Have (2007). As a historical matter, however, Farber's reading of the Ninth Amendment is quite controversial. See Kurt T. Lash, "A Textual-Historical Theory of the Ninth Amendment," Stanford L. Rev. (forthcoming, 2007). Nothing I say in the present book assumes that the Ninth Amendment protects any human rights. Indeed, given section one of the Fourteenth Amendment, whose meaning I explicate in Chapter 4, there is no need to read the Ninth Amendment to protect any human rights.

[41] As I have explained elsewhere, a constitutional doctrine is constitutional bedrock if the doctrine is well-settled and there is no significant support – in particular, among the political elites – for abandoning the doctrine. See Michael J. Perry, We the People: The Fourteenth Amendment and the Supreme Court 19–23 (1999).

[42] For the most impressive argument in support of the claim that the Fourteenth Amendment was meant, inter alia, to make the most important provisions of the Bill of Rights applicable to the states, see

The three post-Civil War Amendments – the Thirteenth, Fourteenth, and Fifteenth Amendments – contain important human rights provisions. According to the Thirteenth Amendment (1866):

> Neither slavery nor involuntary servitude, except as punishment for a crime whereof the party shall have been duly convicted, shall exist within the United States, or any place subject to their jurisdiction.

According to the Fourteenth Amendment (1868):

> No State shall make or enforce any law which shall abridge the privileges or immunities of citizens of the United States; nor shall any State deprive any person of life, liberty, or property, without due process of law; nor deny to any person within its jurisdiction the equal protection of the laws.

According to the Fifteenth Amendment (1870):

> The right of citizens of the United States to vote shall not be denied or abridged by the United States or by any State on account of race, color, or previous condition of servitude.

The other amendments that contain human rights provisions all concern the right to vote. The Nineteenth Amendment (1920) echoes the Fifteenth Amendment:

Michael Kent Curtis, No State Shall Abridge: The Fourteenth Amendment and the Bill of Rights (1986).

> The right of citizens of the United States to vote shall not be denied or abridged by the United States or by any State on account of sex.

According to the Twenty-fourth Amendment (1964):

> The right of citizens of the United States to vote in any primary or other election for President or Vice President, for electors for President or Vice President, or for Senator or Representative in Congress, shall not be denied or abridged by the United States or by any State by reason of failure to pay any poll tax or other tax.

According to the Twenty-sixth Amendment (1971):

> The right of citizens of the United States, who are eighteen years of age or older, to vote shall not be denied or abridged by the United States or by any State on account of age.[43]

[43] Although the human rights provisions of the Constitution protect human beings, so do, in their own, indirect way, the power-allocating provisions of the Constitution: the provisions that allocate power among the three branches of the federal government or between the federal government and the governments of the states. See, for example, J. Harvie Wilkinson III, "Our Structural Constitution," 104 Columbia L. Rev. 1687 (2004).

CHAPTER TWO

Constitutionally Entrenched Human Rights, the Supreme Court, and Thayerian Deference

> Felix Frankfurter described [James Bradley Thayer], his teacher, as "our great master of constitutional law." Thayer, said Frankfurter, "influenced Holmes, Brandeis, the Hands (Learned and Augustus) ... and so forth. I am of the view that if I were to name one piece of writing on American Constitutional Law – a silly test maybe – I would pick an essay by James Bradley Thayer in the *Harvard Law Review*, consisting of 26 pages, published in October, 1893, called 'The Origin and Scope of the American Doctrine of Constitutional Law' ... Why would I do that? Because from my point of view it's a great guide for judges and therefore, the great guide for understanding by non-judges of what the place of the judiciary is in relation to constitutional questions."[1]

[1] Leonard W. Levy, "Editorial Note," in Leonard W. Levy, ed., Judicial Review and the Supreme Court: Selected Essays 84 (1967). Paul Kahn

I explained in the preceding chapter why it makes sense for a liberal democracy to entrench (certain) human rights laws. Whether it also makes sense for a liberal democracy to empower its courts to protect (enforce) the entrenched human rights laws is a separate question. "One can have a constitution of entrenched rules but leave the interpretation of those rules to democratic decision making, and many countries do just that."[2] But why would a liberal democracy choose on the one hand to entrench norms and on the other not to empower its courts to protect the norms? Albert Venn Dicey suggested the answer in *An Introduction to the Study of the Law of the Constitution* (1885): "The restrictions placed on the action of the legislature under the French constitution are not in reality laws, since they are not rules which in the last resort will be enforced by the courts. Their true character is that of

reports that:

> Thayer was a friend and professional colleague of Oliver Wendell Holmes's, first in law practice and then at Harvard, where Thayer taught for thirty years. Louis Brandeis was a student of Thayer's, and Felix Frankfurter, who just missed Thayer at Harvard, acknowledged Thayer's substantial influence. Of Thayer's most famous essay in constitutional law, "The Origin and Scope of the American Doctrine of Constitutional Law," Holmes wrote, "I agree with it heartily and it makes explicit the point of view from which implicitly I have approached the constitutional questions upon which I have differed from some other judges."

Paul Kahn, Legitimacy and History: Self-Government in American Constitutional Theory 84 (1992).

2 Larry A. Alexander, "Constitutionalism," in Martin P. Golding & William A. Edmundson, eds., The Blackwell Guide to the Philosophy of Law and Legal Theory 248, 255 (2004).

maxims of political morality, which derive whatever strength they possess from being formally inscribed in the constitution, and from the resulting support of public opinion."[3] Even if courts are not empowered to protect them (and, indeed, even if courts *are* so empowered), constitutionally entrenched human rights – qua "maxims of political morality" – can serve as shared, fundamental grounds of political-moral judgment in a political community.[4]

Nonetheless, contemporary liberal democracies typically empower their courts to protect constitutionally entrenched human rights.[5] Is it appropriate – is it a good idea, all things

[3] Quoted in James B. Thayer, "The Origin and Scope of the American Doctrine of Constitutional Law, 7 Harvard L. Rev. 129, 130 (1893) (emphasis added).

[4] See Michael J. Perry, Moralty, Politics, and Law 153 et seq. (1988).

[5] Australia and New Zealand are exceptions. For a vigorous argument in defense of the status quo in Australia, see James Allan, "A Defense of the *Status Quo*," in Tom Campbell et al., eds., Protecting Human Rights: Instruments and Institutions 175 (2003). See also James Allan, "Rights, Paternalism, Constitutions and Judges," in Grant Huscroft & Paul Rishworth, eds., Litigating Rights: Perspectives from Domestic and International Law 29 (2002). For an argument in opposition to the status quo in Australia, see Dianne Otto, "Addressing Homelessness: Does Australia's Indirect Implementation of Human Rights Comply with Its International Obligations," in Campbell et al., Protecting Human Rights, supra this note. For an argument that New Zealand ought to establish a system of judicial review, see Andrew S. Butler, "Judicial Review, Human Rights and Democracy," in Huscroft & Rishworth, supra this note, at 47. See also G.W.G. Leane, "Enacting Bills of Rights: Canada and the Curious Case of New Zealand's 'Thin' Democracy," 26 Human Rights Quarterly 152 (2004). But cf. James Allan, "The Effect of a Statutory Bill of Rights where Parliament is Sovereign: The Lesson from New Zealand," in Tom Campbell et al., eds., Sceptical Essays on Human Rights 375 (2001).

considered – for liberal democracies to do so?[6] I have argued elsewhere that the answer is yes; there is no need to rehearse my argument here.[7] The more serious – and more difficult – question is this: How great should the courts' power to protect constitutionally entrenched human rights be; in particular, should it be the power to have the last word when the courts conclude that the law in question violates an entrenched human right (the last word, that is, short of an extremely improbable event: a successful, supermajoritarian effort to amend or repeal the entrenched provision on which the court based its decision)? I have argued elsewhere that the courts' power should not be so great; the judicial power to protect constitutionally entrenched human rights should be the power of judicial "penultimacy," not the power of judicial "ultimacy": the power to have, not the last word, but only the penultimate word – for example, a word that may be overruled by ordinary legislation.[8] Canada, in 1982, and the United

[6] This question is distinct from the question whether it is a good idea, all things considered, for a liberal democracy to empower its courts to protect constitutionally entrenched norms other than human-rights norms, such as, in the United States, separation-of-powers norms (that is, norms allocating power among the three branches of the national government) or federalism norms (norms allocating power between the national government and the governments of the states). See Jesse Choper, Judicial Review and the National Political Process: A Functional Reconsideration of the Supreme Court (1980).

[7] See Michael J. Perry, Toward a Theory of Human Rights: Religion, Law, Courts, 90 et seq. (2007).

[8] See id. at 98–102.

Kingdom, in 1998, each opted for a system (each for a different system) of judicial penultimacy.[9]

In the United States, however, the Supreme Court exercises the power of judicial ultimacy: No state legislature, nor even Congress, may overrule by ordinary legislation a decision by the Court that a law is unconstitutional; such a decision may be overruled only (later) by the Court itself or by extraordinary, supermajoritarian lawmaking, in the form of constitutional amendment.[10] This important question therefore arises:

> Given that the Supreme Court of the United States exercises the power of judicial ultimacy, should the Court, in protecting constitutionally entrenched human rights, exercise the power deferentially? That is, in a case in which it is claimed that a law violates a constitutionally entrenched human right, should the Supreme Court

[9] See id. at 99–101 (Canada) & 113–17 (United Kingdom).

[10] The doctrine of judicial supremacy should not be confused with the different and extremely problematic doctrine of judicial *exclusivity* that the present Supreme Court seems, implicitly, to have embraced. The Court has been acting as if it is not only the supreme but also the exclusive expositor of constitutional meanings. See Larry D. Kramer, "Foreword: We the Court," 115 Harvard L. Rev. 4 (2001); Robert C. Post & Reva B. Siegel, "Protecting the Constitution from the People: Juricentric Restrictions on Section Five Power," 78 Indiana L. J. 1 (2003).

If legislators believe that an existing law is unconstitutional, they may on that basis vote to repeal the law even if the law is not unconstitutional in the Supreme Court's judgment; similarly, if the legislators believe that a proposed law would be unconstitutional, they may on that basis decline to enact the law even if in the Court's judgment the law would not be unconstitutional.

> inquire merely whether the counterclaim that the law does not violate the right is reasonable – and if the Court answers yes, uphold the law? Or, instead, should the Court exercise its power nondeferentially; should it determine for itself whether the law violates the right – and if it answers yes, strike down the law?

A claim that a law does not violate a right is reasonable if rational, well-informed, and thoughtful persons could affirm the claim. As James Bradley Thayer put it: "The reasonable doubt . . . of which our judges speak is that reasonable doubt which lingers in the mind of a competent and duly instructed person who has carefully applied his faculties to the question. The rationally permissible opinion of which we have been talking is the opinion reasonably allowable to such a person as this."[11]

The choice here is best understood as a choice between two different judicial attitudes or orientations. For a judge to adopt a *deferential* attitude – for her to be oriented deferentially – is for her to be prepared to rule that a challenged law does not violate a constitutionally entrenched human right if the claim that the law does not violate the

[11] See Thayer, "The Origin and Scope of the American Doctrine of Constitutional Law," n. 3, at 149.

right is reasonable.[12] By contrast, for a judge to adopt a *non-deferential* attitude is for her to be prepared to rule that a challenged law violates a human right if in the judge's own view the law violates the right – even if the claim that the law does not violate the right is reasonable.

The most famous and influential argument for the sort of judicial deference I have in mind was made by James Bradley Thayer in the final decade of the nineteenth century, in an essay in the *Harvard Law Review*: "The Origin and Scope of the American Doctrine of Constitutional Law."[13] Even now, in the first decade of the twenty-first century, Thayer's essay remains the locus classicus of the argument that in the exercise of their great power to protect constitutional norms, the courts – including the Supreme Court – should proceed deferentially:

> [The court] can only disregard the [challenged] Act when those who have the right to make laws have not merely made a mistake, but have made a very clear one – so clear that it is not open to rational question. That is the standard of duty to which the courts bring legislative Acts; that is the test which they apply – not merely their own judgment

[12] See id. at 150: "[A] court cannot always, and for the purpose of all sorts of questions, say that there is but one right and permissible way of construing the constitution."

[13] See n. 3. See generally "One Hundred Years of Judicial Review: The Thayer Centennial Symposium," 88 Northwestern U. L. Rev. 1–468 (1993).

as to constitutionality, but their conclusion as to what judgment is permissible to another department which the constitution has charged with the duty of making it. This rule recognizes that, having regard to the great, complex, ever unfolding exigencies of government, much which will seem unconstitutional to one man, or body of men, may reasonably not seem so to another; that the constitution often admits of different interpretations; that there is often a range of choice and judgment; that in such cases the constitution does not impose upon the legislature any one specific opinion, but leaves open this range of choice; and that whatever choice is rational is constitutional.[14]

[14] Thayer, "The Origin and Scope of the American Doctrine of Constitutional Law," n. 3, at 144.

According to Thayer, the deferential approach is fitting when a federal court reviews, for federal constitutionality, federal action, or when a state court reviews, either for federal constitutionality or for state constitutionality, state action, but not when a federal court reviews, for federal constitutionality, state action, in which case (according to Thayer) a non-deferential approach is fitting. See Thayer, "The Origin and Scope of the American Doctrine of Constitutional Law," n. 3, at 154–55. This distinction makes little sense, however. See Sanford Gabin, Judicial Review and the Reasonable Doubt Test 5 (1980): "[T]he reasonable doubt test should be applied not just to all national legislation but, contrary to Thayer's prescription, to all state legislation as well." Most commentators who discuss Thayer's conception of proper judicial role fail even to note the distinction. See, for example, Alexander M. Bickel, The Least Dangerous Branch: The Supreme Court at the Bar of Politics 35–46 (1962); Wallace Mendelson, "The Influence of James B. Thayer upon the Work of Holmes, Brandeis, and Frankfurter," 31 Vanderbilt L. Rev. 71 (1978); but see Charles L. Black Jr., Decision According to Law 34–35 (1981). Even Thayer's most prominent judicial disciple, Felix Frankfurter, failed to note the distinction – or to heed it. See West Virginia State Board of Education v. Barnette, 319 U.S. 624, 661–62, 666–67 (Frankfurter, J., dissenting) (1943).

In contending for judicial deference – for "the rule of the clear mistake," as Alexander Bickel called it[15] – Thayer did not argue that lawmakers are generally better than judges at resolving constitutional questions. Thayer's argument was simply that in the United States, a democracy, the citizens are supposed to be the ultimate political sovereign, and that they, therefore, not the judiciary, should have final responsibility for answering, through their elected representatives, contested constitutional questions – so long as their answers are reasonable. Otherwise "the people cease to function as the popular sovereign."[16]

Moreover, Thayer argued that in exercising their power to protect constitutional norms non-deferentially, courts would subvert the capacity of the people and their representatives to deliberate about contested constitutional questions

[15] See Bickel, n. 14, at 34–46.

[16] Kahn, n. 14, at 87. For Kahn's commentary on Thayer's argument, see id. at 85–89.

One of the readers of this book for Cambridge University Press wrote that it was unclear whether in my judgment Thayer's argument for judicial deference "is itself an interpretation of the Constitution. If so, the process of interpretation that leads to [Thayer's] position is unexplained.... Is there an originalist or textualist argument for 'Thayerian' deference?" I have not understood Thayer's argument for judicial deference to be – and in this book I do not present Thayer's argument as – an interpretation of the Constitution. Nonetheless, whether there is an originalist argument for Thayerian deference – an originalist argument, that is, for a Thayerian reading of "the judicial power" in Article III of the Constitution – is an interesting question, but not one I address here.

as responsibly as they should. Thayer elaborated the point in a book on John Marshall:

> [T]he exercise of judicial review, even when unavoidable, is always attended with a serious evil, namely, that the correction of legislative mistakes comes from the outside, and the people thus lose the political experience, and the moral education and stimulus that comes from fighting the question out in the ordinary way, and correcting their own errors. The tendency of a common and easy resort to this great function, now lamentably too common, is to dwarf the political capacity of the people, and to deaden its sense of moral responsibility.... [B]y adhering rigidly to its own duty, the court will help, as nothing else can,... to bring the people and their representatives to a sense of their own responsibility.[17]

[17] James Bradley Thayer, John Marshall 106–07, 109–10 (1901). See also Thayer, "The Origin and Scope of the American Doctrine of Constitutional Law," n. 3, at 155–56. Keith Whittington reports:

> As the Supreme Court became increasingly activist in the late nineteenth century, James Bradley Thayer complained that this development "has tended to bereave our legislatures of their feeling or responsibility and their sense of honor.... It is a common saying in our legislative bodies when any constitutional point is raised, 'Oh, the courts will set that right.'" The courts "have often assumed a tone that tended to encourage these views," but Thayer warned that such complacency overlooked "how great is legislative power, and how limited is judicial power."

Keith E. Whittington, Political Foundations of Judicial Supremacy 138 (2007) (quoting James Bradley Thayer, "Constitutionality of Legislation: The Precise Question for a Court," The Nation, April 10, 1884, at 315).

Many modern students of American judicial review have shared Thayer's concern. Alexander Bickel, for example, wrote that "[t]he search must be for a [judicial] function . . . whose discharge by the courts will not lower the quality of the other departments' performance *by denuding them of the dignity and burden of their own responsibility*."[18]

Now, to insist that there is an obvious difference – and, in many cases, a consequential difference – between a judge's asking whether the challenged law violates the right it is claimed to violate and asking whether the claim that the law does not violate the right is reasonable, is not to deny that reasonableness *vel non* – including the reasonableness *vel non* of the claim that the law does not violate the right it is claimed to violate – is a matter of degree. And, of course, we should not expect that every judge exercising Thayerian deference will draw the line between the reasonable and the unreasonable at precisely the same point – or, therefore, vote the same way

[18] Bickel, n. 14, at 24 (emphasis added). Cf. Allan C. Hutchinson, "Waiting for Coraf (or the Beatification of the Charter)," 41 U. Toronto L. J. 332, 358 (1991): "By endlessly waiting for CORAF, we place ourselves *in waiting*; it inculcates a servile and sycophantic attitude in people. Such a practised posture of dependence is anathema to the democratic spirit. It is infinitely better to run the unfamiliar risks of genuinely popular rule than to succumb to the commonplace security of distant authority." For a more recent, but none the less critical, statement by Hutchinson, see Allan C. Hutchinson, "Supreme Court Inc: The Business of Democracy and Rights," in Gavin W. Anderson, ed., Rights & Democracy: Essays in UK-Canadian Constitutionalism 29 (1999).

in a case – as every other judge exercising Thayerian deference. Thayerian deference is not an algorithm; it is, again, a judicial attitude or orientation. (I return to this point, and illustrate it, in the final section of the next chapter.) As one of Thayer's interpreters, Sanford Gabin, explained:

> Thayer's rule, like all guideposts, is not self-applying. Even limited by the rule of administration, judges, like criminal juries, might differ over what constitutes a reasonable doubt; the possibilities, the stuff of which reasonable doubts are made, do not always strike all men, however reasonable, alike. Even under Thayer's rule of administration, then, the freedom and the burden of decisionmaking remain.[19]

Nonetheless, "that freedom is narrowed, and that was Thayer's aim. He sought to reduce the scope of judicial freedom without diminishing the judicial duty and burden of judging."[20]

In articulating the "duty and burden of judging," Thayer wrote: "The ultimate arbiter of what is rational and permissible is indeed always the courts, so far as litigated cases bring the question before them. This leaves to our courts a great and stately jurisdiction. It will only imperil the whole of it if it is sought to give them more. They must not step into the shoes

[19] Gabin, n. 14, at 45–46.
[20] Id. at 46.

of the law-maker…"[21] Should we who are citizens of the United States want the Supreme Court to accede to Thayer's view of proper judicial role and exercise only the "great and stately jurisdiction" he defended? That is, should we want the Court to exercise its power of judicial ultimacy only deferentially; should we want the justices of the Court to defer to the claim that the challenged law does not violate the right it is claimed to violate if the claim is reasonable?[22] Which arrangement, for the United States today, is more likely to serve us better[23]:

> A system of judicial ultimacy in which the Supreme Court is deferential (Thayerian) in the exercise of its power to protect constitutionally entrenched human rights?
>
> Or a system of judicial ultimacy in which the Court exercises its power non-deferentially?

[21] Thayer, "The Origin and Scope of the American Doctrine of Constitutional Law," n. 3, at 152.

[22] I have explained elsewhere why the Thayerian argument for judicial deference has little if any power in the context of a system of judicial penultimacy, such as Canada's. See Perry, Toward a Theory of Human Rights, n. 7, at 105–06.

[23] The qualifier "for the United States" is important. Cf. Richard A. Posner, "Review of Jeremy Waldron, *Law and Disagreement*," 100 Columbia L. Rev. 582, 592 (2000):

> There is no reason to suppose that the issue [whether American-style judicial review is a good idea] should be resolved the same way in two different countries, even countries that share the same language and the same basic legal and political heritage. That depends on all sorts of emprical questions and judgmental imponderables involving the political and legal cultures of the two countries and the career path of judges and legislators in them.

Thus far, my elaboration of Thayerian deference has been relatively abstract: It is far from clear at this point exactly what judicial analysis Thayerian deference would countenance in cases involving contested issues of human rights. The first of my two principal aims in the next part of this book – Chapters 3 through 5 – is to elaborate Thayerian deference more concretely, by modeling the judicial analysis that Thayerian deference, properly understood, would countenance in particular cases. We will then be in a better position to consider the question posed at the end of the preceding paragraph.

And we will be in a better position still to answer the question – to assess the all-things-considered appeal of Thayerian deference – if we know what the implications of Thayerian deference would be for our constitutional law of human rights. My second principal aim in the next part of this book is to illustrate some of those implications. In particular, I explain what Thayerian deference would mean – what its implications would be – for three greatly contested issues: the constitutionality of capital punishment (Chapter 3), the constitutionality of state refusals to extend the benefit of law to same-sex marriage (Chapter 4), and the constitutionality of state bans on pre-viability abortions (Chapter 5). Do the implications of Thayerian deference for those three controversies – the second and third of which, at least, are at the epicenter of our culture wars – cast doubt on the proposition that the Supreme Court, in the exercise of its great power to protect constitutionally entrenched human rights, should practice Thayerian deference? Or, instead, do the implications support the proposition?

In the conclusion to this book (Chapter 6), after having both elaborated Thayerian deference more concretely and illustrated the implications of Thayerian deference for some of our constitutional law of human rights, I return to the question-in-chief:

> In exercising its great power to protect constitutionally entrenched human rights, should the Supreme Court proceed deferentially; that is, in a case in which it is claimed that a law violates a constitutionally entrenched human right, should the Court inquire merely whether the counterclaim that the law does not violate the right is reasonable – and if the Court answers yes, uphold the law? Or, instead, should the Court exercise its power nondeferentially; should it determine for itself whether the law violates the right – and if it answers yes, strike down the law?

A clarification is in order before we move on. Whether a law violates the provision of the constitutional text it is claimed to violate – for example, the Eighth Amendment's cruel and unusual punishments clause – comprises two different questions: (1) What right (or other norm) does the provision entrench? (Or, according to the originalist approach to constitutional interpretation, which I discuss in the next chapter: What right was the provision originally understood to entrench?) (2) Does the law violate the entrenched right? Thayerian deference, as I elaborate and defend it in this book, pertains only to the second question. In most constitutional cases, the serious dispute is less likely to be about what right the provision entrenches than about whether the challenged law violates the right the provision is deemed to entrench. This is *either* because there is no serious doubt, in most constitutional cases, about what right the provision entrenches, *or* because, even if there is a serious doubt, the issue has been settled by longstanding precedent. So in this book I focus on the question whether judges – in particular, Supreme Court justices – should exercise deference in addressing the second question: Should judges ask whether the challenged law violates the entrenched right it is claimed to violate? Or, instead, should they ask only whether it is reasonable to conclude that the law does not violate the right it is claimed to violate?[24]

[24] Cf. Mitchell N. Berman, "Constitutional Decision Rules," 90 Virginia L. Rev. 1, 102–04 (2004): "[Thayerian deference,] if it is to exist, will find a more hospitable home at the level of applying constitutional meaning, not deriving it."

CHAPTER THREE

Capital Punishment

I address two questions in this chapter: Is capital punishment unconstitutional? Should the Supreme Court rule that capital punishment is unconstitutional? The questions should not be confused: Although it doesn't make sense to give an affirmative answer to the latter question unless one also gives an affirmative answer to the former question, it can make perfect sense, as I explain in this chapter, to give an affirmative answer to the former question but a negative answer to the latter question.

I. Originalism, yes; Scalia, no

The Eighth Amendment to the Constitution, which limits state as well as federal power,[1] provides: "Excessive bail shall not be required, nor excessive fines imposed, nor cruel and unusual punishments inflicted." Is capital punishment "cruel and unusual" within the meaning of the Eighth Amendment – and therefore unconstitutional?

The Preamble to the Constitution declares, in part, that "We the People of the United States . . . do ordain and establish this Constitution for the United States of America." The text of the Constitution is *We the People's* text; it is *their* text, *their* written communication of various imperatives. To whom does the Preamble's "We the People" refer? Neither to those who wrote (drafted) the constitutional text (or some part of it) nor even to those elected representatives in the states who voted to ratify the text. Rather, "We the People" refers to the citizens *on whose behalf* the text was written and ratified. The constitutional text is, as the Preamble indicates, *their* text. The text of the Bill of Rights is the text of the People – the citizens – in 1789–91 who, through their elected representatives,

[1] *Furman v. Georgia*, 408 U.S. 238, 239 (1972) (per curiam). Recall that it is now constitutional bedrock that the Fourteenth Amendment makes the most important provisions of the Bill of Rights, including the Eighth Amendment, applicable to the states. See Chapter 1, n. 38.

ratified – who "ordain[ed] and establish[ed]" – the Bill of Rights. The text of the Fourteenth Amendment is the text of the People in 1866–68 who, through their elected representatives, ratified the Fourteenth Amendment. And so on.

So the question whether capital punishment is "cruel and unusual" within the meaning of the Eighth Amendment depends on what "cruel and unusual" meant to the People in 1789–91 who constitutionalized (constitutionally entrenched) the imperative that "cruel and unusual punishments [not be] inflicted." The cruel and unusual punishments clause of the Eighth Amendment is *their* text, it is *their* written communication of an imperative, and we cannot know whether imposition of the death penalty violates *their* imperative not to inflict "cruel and unusual" punishment unless we know what "cruel and unusual" meant *to them*. The now-common name for the People's understanding of what their text meant is the "original" understanding or meaning.[2]

[2] See, for example, Robert H. Bork, The Tempting of America: The Political Seduction of the Law 144 (1990); Vasan Kesavan & Michael Stokes Paulsen, "The Interpretive Force of the Constitution's Secret Drafting History," 91 Georgetown L. J. 1113, 1144–45 (2003); Randy E. Barnett, Restoring the Lost Constitution: The Presumption of Liberty 90–93 (2004); Keith E. Whittington, "The New Originalism," 2 Georgetown J. L. & Public Policy 599 (2004); Ilya Somin, "'Active Liberty' and Judicial Power: What Should Courts Do to Promote Democracy?" 100 Northwestern U. L. Rev. 1827 (2006).

It seems that we're almost all originalists now. See, for example, Jack M. Balkin, "Abortion and Original Meaning," 24 Constitutional Commentary (2007); available at http://ssrn.com/abstract=925558. (But

Unfortunately, nothing in the historical record discloses what the People in 1789–91 likely understood "cruel and unusual" to mean. Consider this report of a colloquy in the U.S. Congress on August 17, 1789, while Congress was debating the proposed Bill of Rights, including the Eighth Amendment:

> Mr. SMITH, of South Carolina, objected to the words "nor cruel and unusual punishments;" the import of them being too indefinite.

see Mitchell N. Berman, "Originalism Is Bunk" (2007), available at http://ssrn.com/abstract=1078933.) However, originalists do not all profess the same version of originalism. Today most originalists profess the version Keith Whittington has called "the new originalism," which is the most defensible version of originalism:

> [T]he new originalism is focused less on the concrete intentions of individual drafters of constitutional text than on the public meaning of the text that was adopted.... It is the adoption of the text by the public that renders the text authoritative, not its drafting by particular individuals. This is not to say that the history of the drafting process is irrelevant – it may provide important clues as to how the text was understood at the time and the meaningful choices that particular textual language embodied – but it is not uniquely important to the recovery of the original meaning of the Constitution. Similarly, the discovery of a hidden letter by James Madison revealing the "secret," true meaning of a constitutional clause would hardly be dispositive to an originalism primarily concerned with what the text meant to those who adopted it. The Constitution is not a private conspiracy.

Whittington, supra, at 610–11.

I explain in this chapter why, assuming Antonin Scalia is an originalist, the version of originalism Scalia professes is not defensible. But is Scalia really an originalist? For a negative answer, see Randy E. Barnett, "Scalia's Infidelity: A Critique of 'Faint-Hearted' Originalism," 75 U. Cincinnati L. Rev. 7 (2006).

> Mr. LIVERMORE. – The clause seems to express a great deal of humanity, on which account I have no objection to it; but as it seems to have no meaning in it, I do not think it necessary. . . .
>
> The question was put on the clause, and it was agreed to by a considerable majority.[3]

Now, we do know that, as Justice William Brennan wrote in 1986, "the language of the eighth amendment was taken from the English Bill of Rights of 1689," but according to Brennan "we do not know why the framers were particularly attracted to that language or, for that matter, exactly what the language signified to the English."[4]

By contrast, law professor John Stinneford has argued that we *do* know exactly what the word "unusual" in the English Bill of Rights signified to the English: "the word 'unusual' was a term of art that referred to government practices that are contrary to 'long usage' or 'immemorial usage.'"[5] Let's assume, for the sake of discussion, that Stinneford is right about what "unusual" meant in the English Bill of Rights of 1689. Stinneford goes on to argue that the framers of the

[3] The Founders Constitution 377 (1987) (House of Representatives, Amendments to the Constitution, 17 August 1789).

[4] William J. Brennan, Jr., "Constitutional Adjudication and the Death Penalty: A View from the Court," 100 Harvard L. Rev. 313, 323 (1986).

[5] John F. Stinneford, "The Original Meaning of 'Unusual': The Eighth Amendment as a Bar to Cruel Innovation," 102 Northwestern U. L. Rev. (forthcoming 2008); available at http://ssrn.com/abstract=1015344.

American Bill of Rights knew what "unusual" meant in the English Bill of Rights and that they intended "unusual" in the Eighth Amendment to mean the same thing.[6] There is reason to doubt that the framers of the American Bill of Rights did in fact know what "cruel and unusual" meant in the English Bill of Rights.[7] But even if we grant to Stinneford that the framers of the Eighth Amendment intended "unusual" in the Eighth Amendment to mean what "unusual" meant in the English Bill of Rights, this problem remains: The issue for an originalist is not what those who drafted the Eighth Amendment – "the framers" – meant by "unusual." The issue, rather, is what "We the People" in 1789–91, on whose behalf the Eighth Amendment was made a part of the Constitution, understood "unusual" to mean.

For an originalist, the question is "not what the Framers or Ratifiers meant or understood subjectively, but what their words would have meant objectively – how they would have been understood by an ordinary, reasonably well-informed user of the language, in context, at the time, within the relevant political community that adopted them."[8] The Preamble

[6] See id.

[7] According to Anthony Granucci, the framers of the Eighth Amendment did not know what "cruel and unusual" meant in the English Bill of Rights. See Anthony F. Granucci, "'Nor Cruel and Unusual Punishments Inflicted': The Original Meaning," 57 California L. Rev. 839, 840 (1969).

[8] Kesavan & Paulsen, n. 2, at 1144–45.

to the Constitution tells us who the true authors of the constitutional text are: not the drafters (framers) but "We the People." "It is the adoption of the text by the public that renders the text authoritative, not its drafting by particular individuals."[9] And there is nothing in the historical record to suggest that the public (We the People) in 1789–91 would have understood – indeed, it is less than clear that even the framers understood – "unusual" in the Eighth Amendment to be "a term of art" that meant just what it meant in the English Bill of Rights a hundred years earlier. It is much more likely that the public would have understand both "cruel" and "unusual" in the Eighth Amendment to mean what Samuel Johnson's *A Dictionary of the English Language*, first published in 1756, tells us those two words were conventionally understood to mean at the time.[10] In volume 1, at page 250, "cruel" is defined as: "1. Pleased with hurting others; inhuman; hard-hearted;

[9] See n. 2 (Whittington). I concur in what Stanley Fish says about texts, including legal texts. But Fish goes astray in thinking that the drafters of the Constitution, rather than "We the People," are the authors of the constitutional text. See Stanley Fish, "Intention Is All There Is: A Critical Analysis of Aharon Barak's *Purposive Interpretation in Law*," 29 Cardozo L. Rev. 1109 (2008).

[10] Johnson's dictionary was "the standard authority at the time when the Constitution was drawn up in 1787." Andrew O'Hagan, "Word Wizard," New York Rev. Books, April 27, 2006, at 12, 12 (quoting and reviewing Henry Hitchings, Defining the World: The Extraordinary Story of Dr. Johnson's Dictionary (2006)). Johnson's dictionary "is a beautiful read, and its influence is unending . . . Without it, English-speakers would not be English-speakers as we think of them . . ." Id.

barbarous. 2. [Of things.] Bloody; mischievous; destructive." In volume 2, at page 503, "unusual" is defined as: "Not common; not frequent; rare."

Few would deny that the Eighth Amendment bans any punishment that is *intrinsically* barbaric: barbaric *in and of itself*, no matter how heinous the crime, how culpable the criminal, or how effectively the punishment would deter. (Torture is the paradigmatic example of such a punishment.)[11] Intrinsically barbaric punishment is "cruel" within the meaning of the Eighth Amendment; such punishment is also (we may assume) "unusual" in the sense of "not common; not frequent; rare" – not common, that is, as an officially sanctioned punishment. However, the Eighth Amendment, which declares that "*excessive* bail shall not be required, nor *excessive* fines imposed" (emphasis added), bans more than just intrinsically barbaric punishment. Both individually and cumulatively, the emphasis in the Eighth Amendment on "excessive" and the ordinary meaning of "cruel" support the conclusion that a punishment is "cruel," within the meaning of the Eighth Amendment, not only if it is intrinsically barbaric but also if it goes well beyond what

[11] Torture is sometimes used not as punishment but as a means of getting information. For a discussion of the morality of torture used as a means of getting information, see Patrick Lee, "Interrogational Torture," 51 American J. Jurisprudence 131 (2006).

is necesssary – if it is significantly harsher than necessary – to serve the legitimate aims of punishment.[12] All serious punishment is harsh; the question is whether a punishment is harsher than necessary – *significantly* harsher, not marginally or trivially harsher – and, in that sense, "cruel."[13]

What was the point, then, of adding "and unusual"? Wouldn't it have been enough to ban the imposition just of "cruel" punishments? One important way to test whether a

[12] As early as 1910, the Supreme Court endorsed the position that the cruel and unusual punishments clause "was directed not only against punishments which inflict torture, 'but against all punishments which, by their excessive length or severity, are greatly disproportioned to the offenses charged.'" Weems v. United States, 217 U.S. 349, 367 (1910). Almost a century later, the Court wrote that "[t]he Eighth Amendment succinctly prohibits '[e]xcessive' sanctions." Atkins v. Virginia, 536 U.S. 304, 311 (2002). See also Roper v. Simmons, 543 U.S. 551, 560 (2005): "[T]he Eighth Amendment guarantees individuals the right not to be subjected to excessive sanctions. The right flows from the basic "'precept of justice that punishment for crime should be graduated and proportioned to [the] offense.'" (Quoting Weems v. United States, 217 U.S. 349, 367 (1910).)

[13] See Benjamin Wittes, "What Is 'Cruel and Unusual'?" Policy Review, December 2005 and January 2006:

> The hallmark of cruelty . . . is the needless infliction of pain and suffering. Judging whether a punishment is cruel, therefore, requires an assessment of whether the suffering it entails is necessary for some legitimate government purpose or whether it is senseless. On its face, this inquiry is not a complicated one: A punishment reasonably tied to the goal of deterrence or disabling a criminal from further harm to society is not cruel, however unpleasant it may be. A punishment that goes beyond these goals to wanton violence, irrational harshness, gross disproportionality, or needlessly degrading humiliation can reasonably be described as cruel for constitutional purposes. The essential quality of the cruelty, in other words, is that the punishment in question goes somehow beyond any reasonable punitive purpose.

punishment that one believes (or is inclined to believe) is cruel is in fact cruel – whether it is in fact intrinsically barbaric or, at least, significantly harsher than necessary to serve the legitimate aims of punishment – is to inquire whether the punishment is "unusual": not commonly used for any crime or, at least, for the sort of crime at issue, or for the sort of criminal (for example, a minor).[14] That a punishment is "unusual" in the sense of "not commonly used" is probative – not determinative, but probative – of whether the punishment is in fact "cruel." The thought here is that if a punishment is not "unusual" – if, to the contrary, the punishment is commonly used – it is less likely that the punishment is in fact either intrinsically barbaric or significantly harsher than necessary to serve the legitimate aims of punishment. According to the Eighth Amendment, then, a punishment is not unconstitutional unless it is both "cruel and unusual": either intrinsically barbaric or significantly harsher than necessary *and evidenced as such by the fact that the punishment is not commonly used*.[15]

[14] Cf. Trop v. Dulles, 356 U.S. 86, 100 n. 32 (1958): "If the word 'unusual' is to have any meaning apart from the word 'cruel,' however, the meaning should be the ordinary one, signifying something different from that which is generally done."

[15] As a real-world matter, it is difficult to identify a punishment that is intrinsically barbaric – and in that sense "cruel" – that is not also "unusual" (that is, unusual as an officially and publicly authorized punishment).

Why ban "cruel and unusual punishments," thus understood? Because such punishments are inhumane – they treat human beings inhumanely. In the vocabulary of the morality of human rights, "cruel and unusual punishments" violate human beings; they treat human beings as if they lack inherent dignity. To inflict on a human being a punishment that, even if not intrinsically barbaric, is significantly harsher than necessary to serve the legitimate aims of punishment is to treat him inhumanely; it is to violate him. "The infliction of a severe punishment by the State cannot comport with human dignity ... [i]f there is a significantly less severe punishment adequate to achieve the purposes for which the punishment is inflicted ..."[16]

Given this construal of "cruel and unusual punishments," and even if capital punishment is not intrinsically barbaric,[17] the Eighth Amendment forbids government to inflict capital punishment for, say, the crime of stealing a loaf of bread.[18] In

[16] Furman v. Georgia, 408 U.S. 238, 279 (1972) (Brennan, J., concurring) (internal citation omitted).

[17] See In re Kemmler, 136 U.S. 436, 447 (1890): "Punishments are cruel when they involve torture or a lingering death; but the punishment of death is not cruel, within the meaning of that word as used in the Constitution. It implies there is something inhuman and barbarous, something more than a mere extinguishment of life."

[18] See Marc L. Miller & Ronald F. Wright, Criminal Procedures: Cases, Statutes, and Executive Materials 190–91 (2003): "In Coker v. Georgia, 433 U.S. 584 (1977), the Supreme Court struck down the death penalty as a sentencing option in the rape of an adult woman; ... the constitutional basis for the decision was the Eighth Amendment's prohibition

recent years, the United States Supreme Court has ruled that the Eighth Amendment forbids government to inflict capital punishment on anyone who is retarded[19] or was not yet eighteen when he committed the crime.[20] The question I address here is whether the Eighth Amendment's ban on "cruel and unusual punishments" forbids government to inflict capital punishment on anyone for any crime, *even if capital punishment is not intrinsically barbaric*.

For Justice Antonin Scalia and many others, the question is easy – and the answer is no. Like Robert Bork before him,[21] Scalia argues that the People who constitutionalized the cruel and unusual punishments clause did not think they were thereby banning capital punishment. Therefore, argues Scalia, the Eighth Amendment as originally understood does

of cruel and unusual punishments. Since then only murder convictions have led to death sentences." However, the Supreme Court of Lousiana ruled in 1996 that the death penalty is not excessive for rape of a child under twelve. State v. Wilson, 685 So.2d 1063, 1070 (La. 1996). See John Gibeaut, "A Deal with Death: More States Make Child Molestation a Crime, and Face Likely Challenges," ABA Journal, January 2007, at 12:

> No one in the United States has been put to death for a crime other than murder since 1964. But if the state of Louisiana has its way, convicted child rapist Patrick O'Kennedy would become the first inmate in more than four decades to be executed for a crime in which no victim was killed. The state supreme court is expected to decide Kennedy's fate [in 2008].

19 See Atkins v. Virginia, 536 U.S. 304 (2002).

20 See Roper v. Simmons, 543 U.S. 551 (2005).

21 See Michael J. Perry, The Constitution in the Courts: Law or Politics? 45–46 (1994).

not ban capital punishment.[22] Scalia's "therefore" is a non sequitur.

Scalia is right that the People who constitutionalized the cruel and unusual punishments clause did not think they were thereby banning capital punishment. Indeed, the due process clause of the Fifth Amendment, which became a part of the Constitution at the same time the Eighth Amendment became a part (1791), and the due process clause of the Fourteenth Amendment, which became a part of the Constitution in 1868, both state that government may not deprive a person of life without due process of law. Moreover, the grand jury clause of the Fifth Amendment states that government may not prosecute a person for a "capital" crime – a crime for which the penalty of death may be inflicted – unless a grand jury authorizes it to do so. Clearly, then, the People who made the Fifth and Eighth Amendments a part of the Constitution, like the People who made the Fourteenth Amendment a part of the Constitution, assumed that government may inflict capital punishment (albeit, subject to certain specified constraints).

However, that the People who made the Eighth Amendment a part of the Constitution did not think they were thereby banning capital punishment – indeed, that they expected capital punishment to continue into the foreseeable future – does

[22] See Antonin Scalia, A Matter of Interpretation: Federal Courts and the Law 46, 132, 145–47 (1997).

not entail that capital punishment is consistent with the cruel and unusual punishments clause.[23] Even if it is not intrinsically barbaric, capital punishment is *not* consistent with the cruel and unusual punishments clause – the clause *as originally understood* – if:

> no matter what the crime and who the criminal, capital punishment is significantly harsher than necessary to serve the legitimate aims of punishment; and as evidence that it is significantly harsher than necessary, capital punishment is not commonly used for any crime.

[23] Nor does it entail that the power to impose capital punishment is constitutionally enshrined. See Perry, The Constitution in the Courts, n. 21, at 46 (1994):

> The [People's] expectation that reliance on the death penalty would persist into the future and their decision, given that expectation, to regulate imposition of the death penalty do not constitute a decision to authorize reliance on the death penalty, to *constitutionalize* the death penalty – in that sense, they do not constitute a decision to exempt the death penalty from possible prohibition by the Eighth Amendment.

See also Brennan, n. 4, at 324:

> [The Fifth Amendment] does not, after all, declare that the right of Congress to punish capitally shall be inviolable; it merely requires that when and if death is a possible punishment, the defendant shall enjoy certain procedural safeguards. . . . [W]hat one can fairly say is that they sought to ensure that *if* there was capital punishment, the process by which the accused was to be convicted would be especially reliable.

See generally Shannon D. Gilreath, "Cruel and Unusual Punishment and the Eighth Amendment as a Mandate for Human Dignity: Another Look at Original Intent," 25 Thomas Jefferson L. Rev. 559, 571–84 (2003).

That the People who made the Eighth Amendment a part of the Constitution did not think that in their day capital punishment was signficantly harsher than necessary does not entail that in our day capital punishment is not significantly harsher than necessary. Perhaps today capital punishment is not significantly harsher than necessary to serve the legitimate aims of punishment, but, if so, the reason is not that the People in 1789–91 did not think that in their day capital punishment was significantly harsher than necessary.[24] Similarly, that capital punishment was not "unusual" in 1789–91 – that, to the contrary, capital punishment was *commonly* used in 1789–91 – does not entail that it is not unusual now. Perhaps capital punishment is not unusual now, but, if so, the reason is not that capital punishment was not unusual in 1789–91.

Scalia confuses the imperative the People in 1789–91 constitutionalized – the imperative that "cruel and unusual punishments [not be] inflicted" – with what the People thought, or would have thought, the implications of that imperative to be for capital punishment. It is the imperative that is a part of the Constitution, not the People's thoughts about the implications

[24] See Atkins v. Virginia, 536 U.S. 304, 311 (2002):

> [W]e have read the text of the [Eighth] Amendment to prohibit all excessive punishments. . . . A claim that a punishment is excessive is judged not by the standards that prevailed in 1685 when Lord Jeffreys presided over the 'Bloody Assizes' or when the Bill of Rights was adopted, but rather by those that currently prevail.

of the imperative. Consider the point in a different context. It's a safe bet that the People in 1866–68 who, through their elected representatives, ratified the Fourteenth Amendment did not think they were thereby banning either racially segregated public schooling or anti-miscegenation legislation, each of which persisted into the middle of the twentieth century. But this does not entail that racially segregated public schooling and anti-miscegenation legislation do not violate any of the imperatives the People constitutionalized in ratifying the Fourteenth Amendment. As Keith Whittington has put the point:

> [I]n a defensible version of originalism, authorial expectations about how the text will be applied are not the important measure of textual meaning. It is entirely possible for a text to embody principles or general rules, and much of the constitutional text does exactly that. The point for an originalist should be to understand [what] those original principles or rules [are], to understand what principle was entrenched in the Constitution.[25]

[25] Whittington, n. 2, at 610. See also Andrew Oldenquist, "Retribution and the Death Penalty," 20 U. Dayton L. Rev. 335, 340–43 (2004) (criticizing Scalia's interpretive approach to the Eighth Amendment):

> Scalia points out that the Framers did not think that capital punishment was cruel because they allude to it as an option in the same document in which they prohibit cruel and unusual punishments. But why does it matter whether they thought capital punishment was cruel? What should guide us is what they explicitly prohibit or mandate in the Constitution. And if the Framers' opinions about capital punishment do not count, surely neither do the

Now, this is not to deny what I have emphasized elsewhere: What the People thought, or would have thought, the implications of their constitutionalizing an imperative to be for one or another practice, is probative – not determinative – of what they understood the meaning of their imperative to be.[26]

Again, the most plausible candidate for the original meaning of the cruel and unusual punishments clause is this: *Do not inflict a punishment that is either intrinsically barbaric or significantly harsher than necessary to serve the legitimate aims of*

> opinions of late eighteenth century reasonable bystanders. Where is the evidence that the Framers intended that their own acceptance of capital punishment should determine our interpretation of the Eighth Amendment? And even if they, or the reasonable bystanders of the time, considered burying alive but not hanging to be cruel, it doesn't follow that this is what the Eighth Amendment means or implies. It certainly isn't what it *says*.... Awe at writing a document to guide a new nation through future generations, together with respect for the judgment of future generations, may well have moved them not to want to restrict us by their personal opinions about what is cruel or what is an unreasonable search, and this awe and respect may account for the abtractness of much of the Bill of Rights.

Id. at 341.

[26] See Perry, The Constitution in the Courts, n. 2, at 79–81. See also Whittington, n. 2, at 610–11:

> The scope beliefs that particular drafters might have had about the application of [a] constitutional principle may be useful to understanding what principle they actually intended to convey with their language, but the textual principle should not be reduced to the founders' scope beliefs about that principle. The founders could be wrong about the application and operation of the principles that they intended to adopt.

punishment, as evidenced by the fact that the punishment is not commonly used. If we assume, at least for the sake of discussion, that capital punishment is not intrinsically barbaric, the question whether capital punishment is "cruel and unusual" within the meaning – the *original* meaning – of the Eighth Amendment is the question whether capital punishment is significantly harsher than necessary to serve the legitimate aims of punishment, as evidenced by the fact that the punishment is not commonly used.[27]

II. Significantly harsher than necessary?

> We know enough to say that this or that major criminal deserves hard labor for life. But we don't know enough to decree that he be shorn of his future – in other words, of the chance we all have of making amends.[28]

Is capital punishment significantly harsher than necessary to serve the legitimate aims of punishment? More precisely, in a contemporary liberal democracy, such as the United States,

[27] I would not want to be charged with defending the proposition that capital punishment is intrinsically barbaric; in particular, I would not want to be charged with defending the proposition that no matter what the deterrent effect, capital punishment is barbaric. See Michael J. Perry, Toward a Theory of Human Rights: Religion, Law, Courts, ch. 5 (2007).

[28] Albert Camus, "Reflections on the Guillotine," in Albert Camus, Resistance, Rebellion, and Death 230 (Justin O'Brien, tr., 1974).

is there ever good reason – good *penal* reason – to execute a criminal?

The point of departure, in answering that question, is the morality of human rights, which, as I explained in Chapter 1, holds that every human being has inherent dignity.[29] There is no exception for depraved criminals. The inherent dignity that every human being has is inalienable, according to the morality of human rights; one cannot forfeit one's inherent dignity, no matter how depraved an act one commits. In a recent statement, the United States Conference of Catholic Bishops put it this way:

> Each of us is called to respect the life and dignity of every human being. Even when people deny the dignity of others, we must still recognize that their dignity is a gift from God and is not something that is earned or lost through their behavior. Respect for life applies to all, even the perpetrators of terrible acts. Punishment should be consistent with the demands of justice *and* with respect for human life and dignity.[30]

Why assume, however, that the morality of human rights bears on our analysis of the constitutionalty of capital punishment under the Eighth Amendment? No interpretation of the

[29] Every born human being, that is. See Chapter 1, n. 2.
[30] A Culture of Life and the Penalty of Death: A Statement of the United States Conference of Catholic Bishops Calling for an End to the Use of the Death Penalty 6 (2005).

Eighth Amendment that fails to affirm the morality of human rights – that fails to affirm that every human being has inherent dignity – is even plausible. As Chief Justice Earl Warren emphasized in 1958, in speaking for the Supreme Court, "[t]he basic concept underlying the Eighth Amendment is nothing less than the dignity of man."[31] Almost half a century later, the Supreme Court explained that "[b]y protecting even those convicted of heinous crimes, the Eighth Amendment reaffirms the duty of the government to respect the dignity of all persons."[32] ("All persons" includes even the most depraved criminal. Affirming the morality of human rights, Justice William Brennan once wrote that "even the vilest criminal remains a human being possessed of common human dignity.")[33] The morality of human rights is now a bedrock premise of the constitutional law of the United States, including the Eighth Amendment.

Given that every human being, and therefore every criminal, has inherent dignity, no one ought to execute a criminal

31 Trop v. Dulles, 356 U.S. 86, 100–101 (1958). In 1995, in a case in which the Constitutional Court of the Republic of South Africa declared capital punishment unconstitutional, the president of the court wrote: "Although the United States Constitution does not contain a specific guarantee of human dignity, it has been accepted by the United States Supreme Court that the concept of human dignity is at the core of the prohibition of 'cruel and unusual punishment' by the Eighth and Fourteenth Amendments." State v. Makwanyane and Another, 1995 (6) BCLR 665, 695 (Constitutional Court).

32 Roper v. Simmons, 543 U.S. 551, 560 (2005).

33 Furman v. Georgia, 408 U.S. 238, 273 (1972) (concurring opinion).

unless there is a sufficiently weighty justification for doing so. In the absence of a sufficiently weighty justification, to opt for capital punishment over non-lethal but severe punishment – non-lethal but severe punishment *that offers the possibility of rehabilitation* – would be to treat those who are executed as if they lack inherent dignity. "As I live – declares the Lord Yahweh – I do not take pleasure in the death of the wicked but in the conversion of the wicked who changes his ways and saves his life." (Ezekiel 33:11.)[34] In the absence of a sufficiently

[34] Jeffrie Murphy writes:

> In a letter to Marcellinus, the special delegate of the Emperor Honorius to settle the dispute between Catholics and Donatists, Augustine is concerned with the punishment to be administered for what must have, to him, seemed the most vicious of crimes: the murder of one Catholic priest and the mutilation of another by members of a radical Donatist faction.

Jeffrie G. Murphy, Getting Even: Forgiveness and Its Limits 109 (2003). Murphy then quotes from Augustine's letter:

> I have been a prey to the deepest anxiety for fear your Highness might perhaps decree that they be sentenced to the utmost penalty of the law, by suffering a punishment in proportion to their deeds. Therefore, in this letter, I beg you by the faith which you have in Christ and by the mercy of the same Lord Christ, not to do this, not to let it be done under any circumstances. For although we [bishops] can refuse to be held responsible for the death of men who were not manifestly presented for trial on charge of ours, but on the indictment of officers whose duty it is to safeguard the public peace, we yet do not wish that the martyrdom of the servants of God should be avenged by similar suffering, as if by way of retaliation.... We do not object to wicked men being deprived of their freedom to do wrong, but we wish it to go just that far, so that, without losing their life or being maimed in any part of their body, they may be restrained by the law from their mad frenzy, guided into the way of peace and sanity, and assigned to some

weighty justification, to opt for capital punishment over non-lethal but severe punishment (that offers the possibility of rehabilitation) would be to treat those who are executed as if they are what Thomas Aquinas believed some criminals to be: "fall[en] away from *human dignity*, . . . fall[en] somehow into the slavery of the beasts, so that [they] may be disposed of according to what is useful to others."[35]

What is a sufficiently weighty justification for opting to kill a criminal rather than to punish him severely but in a way that allows for the possibility of his rehabilitation as a human being? "Retribution" is a common answer,[36] but it

> useful work to replace their criminal activities. It is true, this is called a penalty, but who can fail to see that it should be called a benefit rather than a chastisement when violence and cruelty are held in check, but the remedy of repentance is not withheld?

Id. at 110. See also David McIlroy, "Oliver O'Donovan and the Tradition of Christian Thought Regarding the Death Penalty," Law & Justice, No. 156 (2006), 37, 41: "In a debate with O'Donovan, the American Pacifist [sic] Ron Sider said, in support of his case: 'One can engage in many forms of non-lethal coercion and at the same time lovingly appeal to the other person as a free moral agent responsible to God to choose to repent and change. When one engages in lethal violence that is impossible.'"

35 E. Christian Brugger, Capital Punishment and Roman Catholic Moral Tradition 173 (2003). See also E. Christian Brugger, "Aquinas and Capital Punishment: The Plausibility of the Traditional Argument," 18 Notre Dame J. L., Ethics & Social Policy 357, 358 et seq. (2004). For a magisterial history of Western – in particular, Christian – thinking about capital punishment, see James J. Megivern, The Death Penalty: An Historical and Theological Survey (1997).

36 The legitimate aims of punishment are widely understood to be retribution, deterrence, and rehabilitation. See E. Christian Brugger, Capital Punishment and Roman Catholic Moral Tradition 38–56 (2003). Cf. John E. Witte Jr. & Thomas C. Arthur, "The Three Uses of the Law:

is also a misconceived answer. Although retribution tells us that "persons who culpably commit or attempt acts and omissions that are morally wrong deserve punishment,"[37] it does not tell us what punishment they deserve. Imagine someone who has committed a sadistic assault, in the form of torture; that he deserves to be *punished* for his crime – and punished severely – does not entail that he deserves to be *tortured* for his crime. Now imagine someone who has committed a heinous murder; that he deserves to be *punished* for his crime does not entail that he deserves to be *executed* for his crime. "It does not follow from the acceptance of retributive punishment that we must accept the death penalty. How much and what kind of punishment a person deserves don't automatically fall out of a retributive system."[38] Indeed, there are retributivist arguments *against* capital punishment.[39]

A Protestant Source of the Purposes of Criminal Punishment," 10 J. L. & Religion 433, 452–65 (1993–94). Rehabilitation is beside the point in this context; capital punishment is not about rehabilitation.

37 Larry Alexander, "The Philosophy of Criminal Law," in Jules Coleman & Scott Shapiro, eds., The Oxford Handbook of Jurisprudence & Philosophy of Law 815, 816 (2002). For a useful discussion of different kinds of retributive theories of punishment, see Brugger, Capital Punishment and Roman Catholic Moral Tradition, n. 33, at 38–56.

38 Oldenquist, n. 25, at 340.

39 See Robert A. Pugsley, "A Retributivist Argument Against Capital Punishment," 9 Hofstra L. Rev. 1501 (1981); John P. Conrad, "The Retributivist's Case against Capital Punishment," in Ernest van den Haag, ed., The Death Penalty: A Debate 19 (1983); David McCord. "Imagining a Retributivist Alternative to Capital Punishment," 50 Florida L. Rev. 1 (1998); Dan Markel, "State, Be Not Proud: A Retributivist Defense

Again, what is a sufficiently weighty justification for opting to kill a criminal rather than to punish him severely but in a way that allows for the possibility of his rehabilitation as a human being? According to the Catholic Church, no modern society need execute a convicted criminal in order to protect itself from him; section 2267 of the 1997 *Catechism of the Catholic Church* states, in relevant part: "Today, . . . as a consequence of the possibilities which the state has for effectively preventing crime, by rendering one who has committed an offense incapable of doing harm – without definitively taking away from him the possibility of redeeming himself – the cases in which the execution of the offender is an absolute necessity 'are very rare, if not practically non-existent.'" (The words "are very rare, if not practically non-existent" are borrowed from John Paul II's 1995 encyclical *Evangelium Vitae*.)[40] The Church's position on this point seems right.[41] But, still, even a modern society may need to execute some convicted criminals

of the Commutation of Death Row and the Abolition of the Death Penalty," 40 Harvard Civil Rights-Civil Liberties L. Rev. 407 (2005).

40 See Brugger, Capital Punishment and Roman Catholic Moral Tradition, n. 33, at 9–37.

41 It bears mention that incarceration can present serious human rights problems of its own. See, for example, Human Rights Watch, "Out of Sight: Super-Maximum Security Confinement in the United States (2000), www.hrw.org/reports/2000/supermax/; Adam Liptak, "Inmate Was Considered 'Property' of Gang, Witness Tells Jury in Prison Rape Lawsuit," New York Times, September 25, 2005.

in order to protect itself, not from *those* criminals, but from some *other* criminals, or from some would-be criminals. That is, capital punishment might have a deterrent effect; at least, it might have a deterrent effect in *some* societies.[42] And, indeed, some recent economic studies suggest that in the United States, capital punishment does have a deterrent effect.[43]

Nonetheless, it remains a matter of great controversy, to say the least, whether, in the United States generally or in any

[42] In this chapter, by deterrence I mean marginal deterrence. See Robert Weisberg, "The Death Penalty Meets Social Science: Deterrence and Jury Behavior Under New Scrutiny," 1 Annual Rev. L. & Social Science 151, 152 (2005):

> [O]ther things being equal, the presence or enforcement of the death penalty obviously will produce fewer homicides than not punishing homicides at all. Thus, the question is one of *marginal* deterrence – i.e., whether the death penalty deters more homicides than the next most severe penalty, which in all jurisdictions [in the United States] is some form of life imprisonment, and in most of the relatively new sentence of life without the possibility of parole. So it is solely for convenience that throughout this review deterrence stands for marginal deterrence.

[43] In one study, for example, the three co-authors – one of whom is my Emory colleague, economist Joanna Shepherd – conclude "that capital punishment has a strong deterrent effect; each execution results, on average, in 18 fewer murders – with a margin of error of plus or minus 10. Tests show that results are not driven by tougher sentencing laws, and are also robust to many alternative specifications." The quoted language is from the abstract of the article: Hashem Dezhbakhsh, Paul H. Rubin, & Joanna M. Shepherd, "Does Capital Punishment Have a Deterrent Effect? New Evidence from Post-Moratorium Panel Data," 5 American Law & Economics Rev. 344 (2003).

state, capital punishment does in fact have a deterrent effect.[44]

[44] See John Donohue & Justin Wolfers, "Uses and Abuses of Empirical Evidence in the Death Penalty Debate," 58 Stanford L. Rev. 791, 794 (2005) (reviewing the Dezhbakhsh/Rubin/Shepherd study cited in n. 43 and concluding that "the existing evidence for deterrence is surprisingly fragile . . .). See also Richard Berk, "New Claims About Executions and General Deterrence: Deja Vu All Over Again?" 2 J. Empirical Legal Studies 303 (2005); Jeffrey Fagan, Deterrence and the Death Penalty: A Critical Review of the New Evidence, Testimony to the New York State Assembly Standing Committee (January 21, 2005), www.deathpenaltyinfo.org/FaganTestimony.pdf; Jeffrey Fagan, "Death and Deterrence Redux: Science, Alchemy and Causal Reasoning on Capital Punishment," 4 Ohio St. J. Criminal L. 255 (2006); Rudolph J. Gerber, "Economic and Historical Implications for Capital Punishment Deterrence," 18 Notre Dame J. L., Ethics & Public Policy 437 (2004); Lawrence Katz, Steven D. Levitt & Ellen Shustorovich, "Prison Conditions, Capital Punishment, and Deterrence," 5 American L. & Econ. Rev. 318 (2003); Weisberg, n. 42.

One recent economic study, by Joanna Shepherd – more recent than the one by Shepherd and her colleagues cited in n. 43 – concludes that in several states, capital punishment not only has no deterrent effect but, perversely, has what she calls a "brutalization effect," increasing the number of murders:

> The results are striking. Consider the twenty-seven states where at least one execution occurred during the sample period. Executions deter murder in only six states. Capital punishment, however, actually *increases* murder in thirteen states, more than twice as many as experience deterrence. In eight states, capital punishment has no effect on the murder rate. That is, executions have a deterrent effect in only twenty-two percent of states. In contrast, executions induce additional murders in forty-eight percent of states. In seventy-eight percent of states, executions do not deter murder.

Joanna M. Shepherd, "Deterrence versus Brutalization: Capital Punishment's Differing Impacts Among States," 104 Michigan L. Rev. 203, 205 (2005). See id. at 205–06:

> [O]n average, the states where capital punishment deters murder execute many more people than do the states where capital punishment incites crime or has no effect. Using various statistical techniques, I show that a threshold number of executions for

Consider in particular the 2005 important Donohue/Wolfers study, which concludes that

> the existing evidence for deterrence is surprisingly fragile . . . Our key insight is that the death penalty – at least as it has been implemented in the United States [in the last thirty years] – is applied so rarely that the number of homicides it can plausibly have caused or deterred cannot be reliably disentangled from the large year-to-year changes in the homicide rate caused by other factors. Our estimates suggest not just "reasonable doubt" about whether there is any deterrent effect of the death penalty, but profound uncertainty. We are confident that the effects are not large, but we remain unsure even of whether they are positive or negative. The difficulty is not just one of statistical significance: whether one measures positive or negative effects of the death penalty is extremely sensitive to very small changes in econometric specifications. Moreover, we are pessimistic that existing data can resolve this uncertainty.[45]

deterrence exists, which is approximately nine executions during the sample period. In states that conducted more executions than the threshold, executions, on average, deterred murder. In states that conducted fewer executions than the threshold, the average execution increased the murder rate or had no effect.

Id.

[45] Donohue & Wolfers, n. 44, at 795. See also id. at 841–45. See also John J. Donohue & Justin Wolfers, "The Death Penalty: No Evidence for Deterrence," Economists' Voice, April 2006, www.bepress.com/ev; New Jersey Death Penalty Study Commission Report 24–26 (January 2007).

Clearly, we may reasonably doubt that capital punishment has a deterrent effect. Strikingly, "[e]ven those on the front lines of crime are skeptical about the deterrent effect of capital punishment. In a 1995 study of 386 randomly selected police chiefs, two-thirds of them said the death penalty didn't significantly reduce the number of homicides."[46] Moreover, "[a] 1996 survey of criminology experts – past and current presidents of three criminology associations – also rejected the notion that executions deter. More than 87 percent believed that the death penalty had no deterrent effect . . ."[47]

Unless it has a deterrent effect, capital punishment is significantly harsher than necessary to serve the legitimate aims of punishment. Even if, like the police chiefs and criminology experts, we reject the claim that capital punishment has a deterrent effect – even if we believe that capital punishment

[46] Editorial, "No Airtight Case for Death," Birmingham [Alabama] News, November 10, 2005, at 8A. This editorial is one in a recent six-part series in which the editorial page of the Birmingham News came out in opposition to use of the death penalty in Alabama. See id.:

> The truth is that there is no proof that the death penalty deters – or that it doesn't. Deterrence supporters can argue that the murder rate would be even higher in states with the death penalty if they didn't use it, just as detractors can point to high murder rates seemingly corresponding to high use of the death penalty. There's no way to show cause and effect. But most data do suggest that there's plenty of reason to doubt the death penalty's ability to deter other murders.

[47] Id. (citing study by University of Florida sociologists Michael L. Radelet and Ronald L. Akers).

does not have a deterrent effect – our belief may be less secure, more tentative, than we would like. After all, the importance of reaching the most careful conclusion we possibly can is profound: Depending on the conclusion we reach, people who would otherwise die may live, or people who would otherwise live may die. How, then, might we test our belief that capital punishment does not have a deterrent effect and is therefore "cruel": significantly harsher than necessary to serve the legitimate aims of punishment?

III. Not commonly used?

Recall the point of adding "and unusual" to "cruel" in the Eighth Amendment: An important way to test whether a punishment that one believes, or is inclined to believe, is cruel is in fact cruel – whether it is in fact significantly harsher than necessary to serve the legitimate aims of punishment – is to inquire whether the punishment is "unusual": not commonly used for the sort of crime at issue, or perhaps for any crime, or for the sort of criminal (for example, a minor). That a punishment is "unusual" in the sense of "not commonly used" is probative of whether the punishment is in fact "cruel"; if a punishment is not "unusual" – if, to the contrary, the punishment is commonly used – it is less likely that the punishment is in fact significantly harsher than necessary.

According to the Eighth Amendment, then, a punishment is not unconstitutional unless it is both "cruel and unusual": significantly harsher than necessary to serve the legitimate aims of *punishment and evidenced as such by the fact that the punishment is not commonly used.*

Is capital punishment "unusual" – is it "not commonly used" – in the United States at this time? Twelve states and the District of Columbia have abolished capital punishment. The abolitionist states include Massachusetts, Michigan, Minnesota, and Wisconsin. Thirty-eight states, the U.S. government, and the U.S. military still allow the death penalty (although in 2004, the death penalty was invalidated on the basis of the state constitution in both New York and Kansas).[48] To maintain the death penalty on the books is not necessarily to use the death penalty, or to use it very often.[49]

[48] Cf. Franklin E. Zimring, "The Unexamined Death Penalty: Capital Punishment and Reform of the Model Penal Code," 105 Columbia L. Rev. 1396, 1409 (2005): "In some Southern states, inadequate defense and appellate lawyers and judges willing to use procedural defaults to nullify substantive legal claims have created much higher rates. For example, Virginia's, Texas's, and Missouri's rates of execution are more than thirty times those of Ohio, Pennsylvania, and California."

[49] The Supreme Court began a four-year moratorium on capital punishment in 1972 (see Furman v. Georgia, 408 U.S. 238 (1972)) and ended it four years later (see Gregg v. Georgia, 428 U.S. 153 (1976)). ("The Supreme Court's decision in *Furman* effectively declared unconstitutional the death penalty statutes then in place in 40 states and commuted the sentences of 629 death row inmates around the country. Because only Justices Brennan and Marshall asserted that the death penalty was per se unconstitutional, the opinions of Justices Stewart, White, and Douglas suggested that states could rewrite their

Still, it is not plausible to say that in the United States at this time (2008), capital punishment is "not commonly used."[50]

However, we need not – indeed, we should not – confine our inquiry to the United States: Is capital punishment "unusual" among the liberal democracies of the world?[51] (I assume it needs no argument that the practice of liberal democracies – democracies that take seriously the claim that every human being has inherent dignity – is the relevant measure, not the practice of dictatorships and fundamentalist theocracies.) Given why we're asking the question ("Is capital punishment 'unusual'?") in the first place, it would make no sense at all to confine our inquiry to the United States. If every liberal democracy in the world except the United States had abolished capital punishment, wouldn't this be probative

death penalty statutes to remedy the constitutional problems." Miller & Wright, n. 7, at 184–85.) In the more than thirty years since the moratorium ended, the following states have executed fewer than five persons (the number executed is in parentheses): Colorado (1), Connecticut (1), Idaho (1), Kansas (0), Kentucky (2), Maryland (4), Montana (2), Nebraska (3), New Hampshire (0), New Jersey (0), New Mexico (1), New York (0), Oregon (2), Pennsylvania (3), South Dakota (0), Tennessee (1), Washington (4), Wyoming (1). In the same period, the U.S. government has executed 3 persons, and the U.S. military, none.

50 Benjamin Wittes has suggested determining the "unusualness" of a punishment by "set[ting] the number of states at three-quarters of the number of states in the Union, currently 38. This corresponds to the number of states required to amend the Constitution." Wittes, "What Is 'Cruel and Unusual'?" n. 13.

51 Cf. Joan F. Hartman, "'Unusual' Punishment: The Domestic Effects of International Norms Restricting the Application of the Death Penalty," 52 U. Cincinnati L. Rev. 655 (1983).

of whether the United States, in continuing to rely on capital punishment, was relying on a punishment significantly harsher than necessary to serve the legitimate aims of punishment? If so, confining our inquiry to the United States would deprive us of the very information we need to test our belief that capital punishment is significantly harsher than necessary. We should cast our net broadly, not because we think that the United States should follow the moral lead of other liberal democracies, but because what other liberal democracies are doing is probative – not determinative, but probative – of whether what the United States is doing is significantly harsher than necessary and therefore cruel (inhumane).[52]

Which liberal democracies have abolished the death penalty (for all crimes)? The list of abolitionist states, many of which we would recognize as genuine liberal democracies, contains eighty-five countries, including, in addition to our neighbors to the north (Canada) and south (Mexico), Australia, Austria, Belgium, the Czech Republic, Denmark, Finland, France, Germany, Hungary, Ireland, Italy, the Netherlands, New Zealand, Norway, Poland, Portugal, the Slovak Republic, South Africa, Spain, Sweden, Switzerland,

[52] Cf. Roper v. Simmons, 543 U.S. 551, 575 (2005): "Our determination that the death penalty is disproportionate punishment for offenders under 18 finds confirmation in the stark reality that the United States is the only country in the world that continues to give official sanction to the juvenile death penalty."

Turkey, and the United Kingdom. Which liberal democracies have retained the death penalty? The list of retentionist states[53] contains seventy-six countries, a small minority of which are liberal democracies, including India, Japan, South Korea, and the United States of America. Undeniably, then, capital punishment is "unusual" – is "not commonly used" – among the liberal democracies of the world.[54]

Perhaps the deterrent effect of capital punishment is greater in the United States than it was in the liberal democracies that have abolished capital punishment. Perhaps the liberal democracies that have abolished capital punishment, or some significant number of them, have abolished it without regard to its deterrent effect.[55] Unless there is a plausible

[53] The list of retentionist countries excludes twenty-four countries that Amnesty International categorizes as "abolitionist in practice": "countries which retain the death penalty for ordinary crimes such as murder but can be considered abolitionist in practice because they have not executed anyone during the last 10 years and are believed to have a policy or established practice of not carrying out executions. The list also excludes countries that have made an international commitment not to use the death penalty."

[54] In 2004, there were at least 3,797 executions in twenty-five countries around the world. China, Iran, the United States, and Vietnam were responsible for 94 percent of these known executions: China (at least 3,400 executions), Iran (approximately 159), Vietnam (approximately 64), and the United States (59). The next four were Saudi Arabia (33), Pakistan (15), Kuwait (9), and Bangladesh (7). Id.

[55] Cf. Youngjae Lee, "International Consensus as Persuasive Authority in the Eighth Amendment," 56 U. Pennsylvania L. Rev. 63, 115 (2007): "That there is an overwhelming consensus ceases to be so impressive unless the Court is able to show each country has converged on the same conclusion for the same reason and that the same reason is also important to us."

argument that one or both of those possibilities is true, however – I am unaware of such an argument – the fact that capital punishment is unusual among the liberal democracies of the world strongly supports our belief that in the United States, capital punishment does not have a deterrent effect and is therefore "cruel": significantly harsher than necessary to serve the legitimate aims of punishment.

IV. Should the Supreme Court rule that capital punishment is unconstitutional

I said at the beginning of this chapter that although it doesn't make sense to conclude that the Supreme Court should rule that capital punishment is unconstitutional unless one also concludes that capital punishment is unconstitutional, it can make perfect sense to conclude that capital punishment is unconstitutional while at the same time concluding that the Supreme Court should not so rule. Let me explain.

Is capital punishment unconstitutional? I have presented an argument in support of an affirmative answer. However, to say that capital punishment is unconstitutional is not to deny that one can reasonably conclude that capital punishment is not unconstitutional. Nor is it to say that the Supreme Court should rule that capital punishment is unconstitutional. Whether capital punishment is unconstitutional and whether the Supreme Court should rule that capital punishment is unconstitutional are different questions. The answer to the latter question depends on the answer to this inquiry: Should the Supreme Court of the United States inquire merely whether the claim that capital punishment is not "cruel and unusual" is reasonable – and if the Court answers yes, uphold the law authorizing capital punishment? Or, instead, should the Court determine for itself whether capital punishment is "cruel and unusual" – and if it answers yes, strike down the law? The argument for Thayerian deference is an argument for the Court's taking the former path rather than the latter one. What are the the implications of Thayerian deference for the controversy over the constitutionality of capital punishment?

I have explained in this chapter why one can reasonably conclude that even if capital punishment is not intrinsically barbaric, it now violates one of the principal human rights provisions of the United States Constitution – namely, the Eighth Amendment's ban on punishment that is *significantly harsher than necessary to serve the legitimate aims of punishment, as evidenced by the fact that the punishment is not commonly used.*[56] I have not argued, however, that one cannot

[56] *The New Jersey Death Penalty Study Commission* Report (January 2007) found that "[t]here is no compelling evidence that the New Jersey death penalty rationally serves a legitimate penological intent."

reasonably reject that conclusion. Whether one can reasonably reject it depends ultimately on whether one can reasonably affirm either of the following two propositions. (In what follows, "Texas" stands for whatever state it is whose system of capital punishment is at issue.)[57]

1. In Texas (or in the United States, if the federal system is at issue), capital punishment has, or probably has, a deterrent effect.
2. Although it is uncertain whether in Texas capital punishment has a deterrent effect, Texas legislators may resolve the benefit of the doubt in favor of the assumption that it *does* have a deterrent effect; that is, they may resolve the benefit of the doubt in favor of protecting the lives of the innocent rather than the lives of those who are guilty of a heinous crime. The legislators must choose, and in choosing they may give the benefit of the doubt to the innocent.

The *Report* also found that "[t]he alternative of life imprisonment in a maximum security institution without the possibility of parole would sufficiently ensure public safety and address other legitimate social and penological interests, including the interests of the families of murder victims." See pp. 24–30, 56–61.

[57] Cf. Editorial, "No Airtight Case for Death," The Birmingham News, November 10, 2005, at 8A: "Texas ... accounts for more than a third of all executions in the United States. Last year [2004], it carried out 23 of the 59 executions in the country; no other state approached double figures."

If one can reasonably affirm either proposition, then one can reasonably conclude that in Texas, capital punishment is not significantly harsher than necessary and therefore does not violate the Eighth Amendment. So, can one reasonably affirm either proposition? I am inclined to answer yes, but be that as it may, the important point, for present purposes, is this: The question a Supreme Court justice committed to Thayerian deference would ask himself is not whether in Texas capital punishment (probably) has a deterrent effect, but only whether one can reasonably conclude *either* that it does *or* that the benefit of the doubt may be resolved in favor of protecting the innocent.

Let's assume that there *is* room for a reasonable difference in judgments about whether capital punishment is "cruel and unusual" within the meaning of the Eighth Amendment – and that, *pace* Thayer, the Supreme Court should not rule that capital punishment violates the Eighth Amendment. Is there also room for a reasonable difference in judgments about whether inflicting capital punishment *on the mentally retarded, or on minors* (that is, those who were not yet eighteen when they committed their crime), is "cruel and unusual"? Even if one thinks that *some* capital punishment may have a deterrent effect, isn't it implausible to think that the deterrent effect that some capital punishment may have would be diminished by the abolition of capital punishment either for the mentally retarded or for minors?[58] If so, then there

[58] The Supreme Court has addressed this issue. See Atkins v. Virginia, 536 U.S. 304, 319–20:

> With respect to deterrence – the interest in preventing capital crimes by prospective offenders – it seems likely that capital punishment can serve as a deterrent only when murder is the result of premeditation and deliberation. [The] same cognitive and behavioral impairments that make [the mentally retarded] morally less culpable – for example, the diminished ability to understand and process information, to learn from experience, to engage in logical reasoning, to control impulses – . . . also make it less likely that they can process the information of the possibility of execution as a penalty and, as a result, control their conduct based upon that information. Nor will exempting the mentally retarded from execution lessen the deterrent effect of the death penalty with respect to offenders who are not mentally retarded. Such individuals are unprotected by the exemption and will continue to face the threat of execution.

See also Roper v. Simmons, 543 U.S. 551, 571–72 (2005) (making a similar point with respect to minors).

Even if one thinks, contrary to what I have argued in this chapter, that there may be a retributive justification for *some* capital punishment, it is implausible to think that there is a retributive justification for executing either the mentally retarded or minors, given each group's significantly diminished moral culpability. The Supreme Court has addressed this issue too. See Atkins v. Virginia, supra this note, at 319:

> With respect to retribution – the interest in seeing that the defender gets his just deserts – the severity of the appropriate punishment necessarily depends on the culpability of the offender. . . . If the culpability of the average murderer is insufficient to justify the most extreme sanction available to the State, the lesser culpability of the mentally retarded offender sure does not merit that form of retribution.

See also Roper v. Simmons, supra this note, at 571:

> Whether viewed as an attempt to express the community's moral outrage or as an attempt to right the balance for the wrong of the victim, the case for retribution is not as strong with a minor as

is no discernible room for a reasonable difference in judgments about whether executing either the mentally retarded or minors is "cruel" in the relevant sense: *significantly harsher than necessary to serve the legitimate aims of punishment*.

Certainly there is no room for a reasonable difference in judgments about whether executing either the mentally retarded or minors is "unusual" in the relevant sense: *not commonly used*. As I have already explained, executing *anyone* is exceedingly rare – because systems of capital punishment are exceedingly rare – in liberal democracies.[59]

So even a Supreme Court stacked to the gills with justices who are committed Thayerians may conclude – and in my view *should* conclude – that the Eighth Amendment forbids "Texas" to execute either the mentally retarded or minors. As it happens, the Supreme Court, though certainly not stacked to the gills with Thayerians, *has* so concluded: in 2002, in *Atkins v. Virginia* (the mentally retarded),[60] and in 2005, in *Roper*

> with an adult. Retribution is not proportional if the law's most severe penalty is imposed on one whose [moral] culpability or blameworthiness is diminished, to a substantial degree, by reason of youth and immaturity.

[59] Moreover, both executions of the mentally retarded and executions of minors were rare in the United States before the Supreme Court ruled that such executions violate the Eighth Amendment. See Atkins v. Virginia, 536 U.S. 304, 313–16 (2002) (mentally retarded); Roper v. Simmons, 543 U.S. 551, 564–67 (minors).

[60] 536 U.S. 304.

v. Simmons (minors).[61] Even from a Thayerian perspective, each ruling is defensible.

Defensible – but not inevitable. I suggested that it is unreasonable to think that the deterrent effect that some capital punishment may have would be diminished by the abolition of capital punishment either for the mentally retarded or for minors. But I suspect that not every judge would agree. Reasonableness *vel non* is a matter of degree, and, as I said in the preceding chapter, we should not expect that every judge exercising Thayerian deference will draw the line between the reasonable and the unreasonable at precisely the same point – or, therefore, vote the same way in a case – as every other judge exercising Thayerian deference. Again, Thayerian deference is not an algorithm; it is only a judicial attitude or orientation. Thayerian deference does not exclude the play of judicial subjectivity from constitutional adjudication; nothing can do *that*.

Nonetheless, Thayerian deference leaves less room for the play of judicial subjectivity than does a non-deferential attitude/orientation. Sanford Gabin explained, in a passage I quoted in the preceding chapter, that

> Thayer's rule, like all guideposts, is not self-applying. Even limited by the rule of administration, judges, like

[61] 543 U.S. 551.

criminal juries, might differ over what constitutes a reasonable doubt; the possibilities, the stuff of which reasonable doubts are made, do not always strike all men, however reasonable, alike. Even under Thayer's rule of administration, then, the freedom and the burden of decisionmaking remain. *But that freedom is narrowed, and that was Thayer's aim*. He sought to reduce the scope of judicial freedom without diminishing the judicial duty and burden of judging.[62]

[62] Sanford Gabin, Judicial Review and the Reasonable Doubt Test 45–46 (1980) (emphasis added).

CHAPTER FOUR

Same-Sex Unions

As we saw in the preceding chapter, one can sensibly conclude that a law (or other policy) violates a constitutionally entrenched human right without also concluding that the Supreme Court should so rule. However, one cannot sensibly conclude that the Supreme Court should rule that a law violates a constitutionally entrenched human right without also concluding that the law violates the right; indeed, from a Thayerian perspective, the Supreme Court should rule that a law violates a constitutionally entrenched human right only if the Court concludes that the claim that the law does not violate the right is unreasonable. In this chapter, I argue that even a Supreme Court committed to Thayerian deference should rule that state refusals to extend the benefit of law to same-sex unions are unconstitutional – because the claim that such refusals are not unconstitutional is not merely mistaken but unreasonable.

Of course, it would be unrealistic (to put it mildly) to expect that any time soon the Supreme Court will rule that state refusals to extend the benefit of law to same-sex unions are unconstitutional. But that doesn't mean that such refusals aren't unconstitutional. In 1896, when *Plessy v. Ferguson*[1] was decided, it would have been unrealistic to expect the Supreme Court to rule that *de jure* racial segregation violated the Fourteenth Amendment.[2] Nonetheless, Justice Harlan was right, in his passionate and prophetic dissent in *Plessy*, that such segregation *did* violate the Fourteenth Amendment.[3]

1 163 U.S. 547.

2 Cf. Richard A. Posner, "Should There Be Homosexual Marriage, And If So, Who Should Decide?" 95 Michigan L. Rev. 1578, 1586 (1997): "When [in 1954] the Supreme Court moved against public school segregation, it was bucking a regional majority but a national minority (white southerners). When [in 1967] it outlawed the laws forbidding racially mixed marriages, only a minority of states had such laws on their books." More recently, Posner wrote that "*Brown [v. Board of Education*, 347 U.S. 483 (1954)] would have been unthinkable – and in my pragmatic view unsound – had the case arisen in 1900 rather than the 1950s, because in 1900 the vast majority of the American population would have considered compelled racial integration of public schools improper." Richard Posner, "Gay Marriage – Posner's Response to Comments," The Becker–Posner Blog, July 24, 2005, http://becker-posner-blog.com.

3 See 163 U.S. at 552–64.

I. The mandate of equal citizenship

Section 1 of the Fourteenth Amendment consists of two sentences, the first of which declares that "[a]ll persons born or naturalized in the United States, and subject to the jurisdiction thereof, are citizens of the United States and of the State wherein they reside." As the Supreme Court emphasized in *The Slaughter-House Cases*, which were decided just four years after ratification of the Fourteenth Amendment was complete, the first sentence of Section 1 was meant to "overturn[] the Dred Scott decision by making *all persons* born within the United States and subject to its jurisdiction citizens of the United States" (and of the state wherein they reside).[4] In *Dred Scott v. Sandford* (1857),[5] which is widely regarded as one of the most indefensible constitutional decisions in American history,[6] the Supreme Court ruled that, as the Court put it fifteen years later, in *Slaughter-House*, "a man of African descent, whether a slave or not, was not and could not be a

[4] Slaughter-House Cases, 83 U.S. (16 Wall.) 36, 73 (1872).
[5] 60 U.S. (19 How.) 393.
[6] See Don E. Fehrenbacher, The Dred Scott Case: Its Significance in American Law and Politics (1978). For a shorter commentary, see Don E. Fehrenbacher, "Dred Scott v. Sandford, 19 Howard 393 (1857)," 2 Encyclopedia of the American Constitution 584 (Leonard W. Levy, Kenneth L. Karst, & Dennis J. Mahoney, eds., 1986).

citizen of a State or of the United States."[7] The *Slaughter-House* Court then stated:

> That [the] main purpose [of the first sentence of section one of the Fourteenth Amendment] was to establish the citizenship of the negro can admit of no doubt. The phrase, 'subject to its jurisdiction' was intended to exclude from its operation children of ministers, consuls, and citizens or subjects of foreign States born within the United States.[8]

Now, the second sentence of Section 1 provides:

> No State shall make or enforce any law which shall abridge the privileges or immunities of citizens of the United States; nor shall any State deprive any person of life, liberty, or property, without due process of law; nor deny to any person within its jurisdiction the equal protection of the laws.

Do state refusals to extend the benefit of law to same-sex unions violate the Fourteenth Amendment? The answer depends on what the second sentence of Section 1 means.

Just as the text of the Eighth Amendment and the rest of the Bill of Rights is the text of the People – the citizens – who in 1789–91, through their elected representatives, ratified – who "ordain[ed] and establish[ed]" – the Bill of Rights, the

[7] 83 U.S. at 73.
[8] Id.

text of the Fourteenth Amendment is the text of the People in 1866–68 who, through their elected representatives, ratified the Fourteenth Amendment. The second sentence of Section 1 is *their* text; it is *their* written communication of three imperatives, and we cannot know whether refusals to extend the benefit of law to same-sex unions violate one or more of *their* three imperatives unless we know what the language of the second sentence of Section 1 meant to *them*.

So, what did the People in 1866–68, who constitutionalized the Fourteenth Amendment, understand the language of the second sentence to mean? I addressed that question at length in my book *We the People: The Fourteenth Amendment and the Supreme Court*; here, I'll simply rehearse my principal conclusions. Readers who are skeptical about my conclusions, or who want more detail, can consult *We the People* and evaluate what I say there.[9]

In the aftermath of the Civil War, it quickly became clear that a state could – and the former Confederate states did – oppress the former slaves, and others, in three different ways. Each of the three clauses (imperatives) of the second sentence of Section 1 responds to one of the three ways – each clause responds to a different way – some state officials might seek to oppress some human beings.

[9] See Michael J. Perry, We the People: The Fourteenth Amendment and the Supreme Court 48–85 (1999).

The due process clause. The People understood the due process clause to forbid state officials to deprive any person of his life, his liberty – that is, his physical freedom – or his property extrajudicially; under the due process clause, state officials may execute a person (life), or imprison him (liberty), or fine him or confiscate his property, if at all, only pursuant to "due process of law", which the People understood to refer to the process of law (the procedural protections) that is generally due citizens and other persons under the state's law. Whether the People understood "due process of law" to refer to more process than that generally due persons under the state's law is neither clear nor, here, relevant.[10]

The equal protection clause. The People understood the equal protection clause to require state officials to give to every person within the state's jurisdiction the same protection ("equal protection") that is generally due persons under the state's law – the same protection "of the laws." What laws? *Protective* laws: laws – such as those against homicide, kidnapping, or theft – that *protect* a person's life, liberty, or property.[11]

The privileges or immunities clause. Even if state officials do not deprive any person of his life, liberty, or property except pursuant to the process that is generally due persons under

[10] See id. at 52–53.
[11] See id. at 54–57.

state law, and even if state officials do not forsake their legal duty to protect every person from those who would unlawfully deprive him of his life, liberty, or property, there is a third way state officials might seek to oppress, and some state officials after the Civil War did oppress, some citizens: by making and enforcing laws that treat some citizens (for example, former slaves) as inferior to other citizens – laws that treat some citizens as second-class citizens (or worse). In forbidding states to "make or enforce any law which shall abridge the privileges or immunities of citizens of the United States . . . ," the People understood themselves to be forbidding states to make or enforce any law that treats some citizens as second-class citizens. The privileges or immunities clause thus complements the first sentence of Section 1: What good would it have done to declare that "[a]ll persons born or naturalized in the United States, and subject to the jurisdiction thereof, are citizens of the United States and of the State wherein they reside" if a state could treat some citizens as second-class citizens?

The privileges or immunities clause does not require states to treat all of their citizens the same. States may treat some citizens less well than other citizens; for example, states may deny driver's licenses to those who are not yet sixteen years of age. However, states may not treat any citizens less well *except pursuant to an exercise of the state's "police" power*: the state's legislative power to serve (protect, secure) the public good. Moreover, under the privileges or immunities clause, a law – a particular instance of treating some citizens less well – does not count as an exercise of the police power if the law – the differential treatment – is based on, and in that sense affirms, the view that those treated less well are second-class citizens, in the sense that they have less dignity (worth, value) than other citizens, or that their interests (their needs and wants) matter less than the interests of other citizens. A law is "based on" a view if but for the view – if in the absence of the view – the law would not have been enacted.

Does a law that discriminates against non-whites – that treats them less well than whites – violate (the privileges or immunities clause of) the Fourteenth Amendment; does it violate, that is, the mandate of equal citizenship? Yes, if the law is based on the racist view that non-whites are, as such, second-class citizens, that they have a lesser dignity than whites, that their interests matter less than the interests of whites. Laws and policies such as those struck down in *Brown v. Board of Education* (*de jure* racial segregation)[12] and *Loving v. Virginia*[13] (anti-miscegenation law) – laws and policies that were aspects or remnants of a system of racial

[12] 347 U.S. 483 (1954).
[13] 388 U.S. 1 (1967).

apartheid – were obviously based on the view that non-whites are second class citizens.[14]

Bolling v. Sharpe,[15] which was a companion case to *Brown v. Board of Education*, involved not *state* action but *federal* action: *de jure* racial segregation in the public schools of the District of Columbia, which is a federal entity. The Supreme Court ruled that although the Fourteenth Amendment does not apply to federal action, the Fifth Amendment due process clause, which does apply to federal action, forbids the federal goverment to engage in discrimination that, were a state to engage in, would violate the Fourteenth Amendment. However, it is a mistake to think that the Fourteenth Amendment does not apply to federal action. The first sentence of Section 1 of the Fourteenth Amendment is as much a limit on federal action as on state action: "All persons born or naturalized in the United States, and subject to the jurisdiction thereof, are citizens of the United States and of the State wherein they reside." And, as I just explained, the privileges or immunities

[14] Similarly, a law that that treats whites less well than non-whites violates the Fourteenth Amendment *if* the law is based on the view that whites are, as such, second-class citizens. I have argued elsewhere that it is not plausible to think that government programs of race-based affirmative action – such as the University of Michigan School of Law program upheld by the Supreme Court in *Grutter v. Bollinger*, 539 U.S. 306 (2003), and the University of Michigan undergraduate program struck down by the Supreme Court in *Gratz v. Bollinger*, 539 U.S. 244 (2003) – are based on any such view. See Perry, We the People, n. 9, at 97–112.

[15] 347 U.S. 497 (1954).

clause of the second sentence was understood to underwrite – to secure – the first sentence by insisting that the citizenship protected by the first sentence is *equal* citizenship. Given the historical context, it is understandable that the second sentence was (and is) directed specifically against state action: "No State shall make or enforce any law which shall abridge the privileges or immunities of citizens of the United States..." Nonetheless, it is undeniably implicit in Section 1 of the Fourteenth Amendment that the federal government, too, and not just state governments, must respect the equal citizenship of all those who are citizens of the United States and of the state wherein they reside.[16] So, in *Bolling*, the Court would have done better to rely not on a non-original meaning of the Fifth Amendment due process clause but on the original meaning of the Fourteenth Amendment privileges or immunities clause. In any event, the Court in *Bolling* was right to declare that "[i]n view of our decision [in *Brown*] that the Constitution prohibits the states from maintaining racially segregated public schools, it would be unthinkable that the same Constitution would impose a lesser duty on the Federal Government."[17]

16 See Akhil Reed Amar, America's Constitution: A Biography 382 (2005).

17 347 U.S. at 500. I want to comment, briefly, on another famous – and famously problematic – decision involving racial discrimination: *Shelley v. Kraemer*, 334 U.S. 1 (1948). See, for example, Mark D. Rosen, "Was *Shelley v. Kraemer* Wrongly Decided? Some New Answers," 95

Again, a law that discriminates against non-whites – that treats them less well than whites – violates the Fourteenth Amendment if the law is based on the view that non-whites are, as such, second-class citizens, that they have a lesser dignity than whites, that their interests matter less than the interests of whites. Similarly, a law that discriminates againt

California L. Rev. 451 (2007). The Fourteenth Amendment's mandate of equal citizenship requires government to respect the equal citizenship of all citizens. Government fails to respect the equal citizenship of all citizens if government treats some citizens as second-class. But government also fails to respect the equal citizenship of all citizens if it either (1) actively enables private (non-governmental) actors to treat some citizens as second-class, or (2) chooses without good reason not to ban private conduct that treats some citizens as second-class. By choosing not to ban private conduct that treats some citizens as second-class, government has not necessarily failed to respect the equal citizenship of all citizens: Whether by choosing not to ban the conduct government has failed to respect the equal citizenship of all citizens depends on whether there is good reason for government not to ban the conduct. In *Burton v. Wilmington Parking Authority*, 365 U.S. 715 (1961), the Supreme Court rightly concluded not only that there was not good reason not to ban the racially discriminatory conduct but that there was compelling reason to ban the conduct. Moreover, even a Thayerian Court could and should have concluded that there was no room for a reasonable difference in judgments about whether there was good reason not to ban the conduct.

Choosing not to ban conduct is one thing; actively enabling conduct is another. It is difficult to imagine a scenario in which government, by actively enabling private actors to treat some citizens as second-class, has not failed to respect the equal citizenship of all citizens. In any event, the facts in *Shelley v. Kraemer* did not constitute such a scenario. So the Court's decision in *Shelley* was correct: By enforcing the racially restrictive covenants at issue in *Shelley*, the California courts had failed to respect – and even a Thayerian Court could and should have concluded that there was no room for a reasonable difference in judgments about whether the California courts had failed to respect – the equal citizenship of those whom the covenants excluded: those "not of the Caucasian race."

women – that treats them less well than men – violates the Fourteenth Amendment if it is based on the view that women are, as such, second-class citizens. A law that discriminates against homosexuals – that treats them less well than heterosexuals – violates the Fourteenth Amendment if it is based on the view that homosexuals are, as such, second-class citizens. And so on.

Sometimes, as in *Brown* and *Loving*, it's clear that a law that treats some citizens – non-whites, women, and so on – less well than other citizens is based on the view that those treated less well are second-class citizens, in the sense that they have less dignity than other citizens, or that their interests matter less than the interests of other citizens. And when it's clear, when there's no fair doubt, that a law represents the view that some citizens are second-class, the case is at an end: States may not treat any citizens as second-class. Period.

When, however, it's not clear, what should a court – and, in particular, the Supreme Court – do? Again, according to the mandate of equal citizenship, states may not treat any citizens less well *except pursuant to an exercise of the state's "police" power*: the state's legislative power "to determine, primarily," as the Supreme Court put it in 1887, "what measures are appropriate or needful for the protection of the public morals, the public health, or the public safety."[18] No law – no instance of differential treatment – is an exercise of the police power unless three conditions are satisfied:

1. The good the differential treatment aims to serve is a *public* good: a good implicating what modern human rights instruments call "public safety, order, health, or morals or the fundamental rights and freedoms of others."[19]

By "the good the differential treatment aims to serve" I mean the good (or goods) the law was originally put on the books to serve – or, if there is a difference, the good the law is now kept on the books to serve. After all, we cannot ascertain whether in putting a law on the books, or in deciding to keep it there, a state has truly exercised its police power until we know why – the real reason for which, the putatively public good for which – the state has put, or kept, the law on the books.

2. The differential treatment actually serves the good it aims to serve.
3. The differential treatment serves the good it aims to serve in a proportionate fashion: The costs the law

[18] Mugler v. Kansas, 123 U.S. 623, 660–61 (1887). See Santiago Legarre, "The Historical Background of the Police Power," 9 U. Pennsylvania J. Const'l L. 745 (2007).

[19] See, for example, Article 18 of the International Covenant on Civil and Political Rights.

imposes on those it treats less well are not so great, so disproportionate, relative to the good the law serves that there is no reasonable justification – no reasonable case to be made – for the differential treatment.[20]

From a Thayerian perspective – which is the perspective of this chapter – the question for a court is not whether in its own judgment the three conditions are satisfied but only whether the claim that the conditions are satisfied is reasonable.[21] A court committed to Thayerian deference should ask whether it is reasonable to conclude that (1) the good the differential treatment aims to serve is a public good, (2) the differential treatment actually serves that good, and (3) it does so in a proportionate fashion. (Recall from Chapter 2 that a conclusion is reasonable if rational, well-informed, and thoughtful persons could reach the conclusion.)[22] If it is unreasonable to regard the good the differential treatment aims to serve as a genuinely public good, or to think that

[20] See Perry, We the People, n. 39, at 57–77. What about "incorporation" of the Bill of Rights? Cf. chapter 1, 39. To put it just a bit oversimply, a state law is not a reasonable exercise of the police power if the law, were it a national (federal) law, would violate the Bill of Rights. See id. at 77–80.

[21] Cf. Stephen Breyer, Active Liberty: Interpreting Our Democratic Constituition 17 (2005): "[A] judge's 'agreement or disagreement' about the wisdom of a law 'has nothing to do with the right of a majority to embody their opinions in law.'" (Quoting Oliver Wendell Holmes's dissenting opinion in *Lochner v. New York*, 198 U.S. 45, 75 (1905).) See also id. at 18–19 (quoting Louis Brandeis, Felix Frankfurter, and Learned Hand to the same effect).

[22] See Chapter 2, n. 11, and accompanying text.

the differential treatment serves that good in a proportionate fashion, then the default conclusion is that the differential treatment is based on the view that those treated less well are second-class citizens.

Even if there were only weak historical (originalist) support for what I have said here about the meaning of the second sentence of section one of the Fourteenth Amendment – in particular, about the meaning of privileges or immunities clause – it is nonetheless constitutional bedrock that the second sentence of section one forbids government to discriminate against any of its citizens – to treat any of them less well than other citizens – on the basis of the view that they are second-class citizens.[23] Just as it is constitutional bedrock, for example, that the Fifth Amendment takings clause applies to the states,[24] even though there may be, at best, only scant historical support for that state of affairs.[25] As Michael McConnell noted recently, "many decisions, even some that were questionable or controversial when rendered, have become part of the fabric of American life; it is inconceivable

[23] See Perry, We the People. n. 9, at 82–87.

[24] See Chicago, B. & Q. R. Co. v. Chicago, 166 U.S. 226 (1897); Kelo v. City of New London, 545 U.S. 469, 472 n. 1 (2005).

[25] See Aviam Soifer, "Text-Mess: There Is No Textual Basis for Application of the Takings Clause to the States," 28 U. Hawaii L. Rev. 373 (2006). A constitutional doctrine is constitutional bedrock if the doctrine is well-settled and there is no significant support – in particular, among the political elites – for abandoning the doctrine. See Perry, We the People, n. 9, at 19–23.

that they would now be overruled.... This overwhelming public acceptance constitutes a mode of popular ratification..."[26] The serious question, then, is not whether government is constitutionally free to discriminate against some of its citizens on the basis of the view that they are second-class citizens, *but whether a law alleged to be based on that view is in fact based on it – and therefore violates the Fourteenth Amendment.*

II. Do state refusals to recognize same-sex unions violate equal citizenship?[27]

Does a law that discriminates against homosexuals violate the Fourteenth Amendment? Yes, if the law is based on the view that homosexuals are, as such, second-class citizens. Such a

[26] Michael W. McConnell, "Active Liberty: A Progressive Alternative to Textualism and Originalism?" 119 Harvard L. Rev. 2387, 2417 (2006).

[27] I don't address in this chapter the question whether the Fourteenth Amendment requires that same-sex unions be recognized as "marriages." On the "marriage" v. "civil unions" issue, compare David S. Buckel, "Government Affixes a Label of Inferiority on Same-Sex Couples When It Imposes Civil Unions & Denies Access to Marriage," 16 Stanford L. & Pol'y Rev. 73 (2005) with Andrew Koppelman, "Civil Conflict and Same-Sex Civil Unions," Responsive Community, Spring/Summer 2004, at 20. In *Lewis v. Harris*, 908 A.2d 196 (NJ 2006), the New Jersey Supreme Court was unanimous in ruling that under the state constitution, all the benefits (and responsibilities) of civil marriage must be extended to same-sex unions, but divided four to three over whether the title "marriage" must be extended to same-sex unions, with the majority declining to take that extra step. Cf. Adam Liptak, "Caution in Court for Gay Rights Groups," New York Times, November 12, 2004.

view is scarcely unfamiliar to us. Richard Posner has written of the "irrational fear and loathing of" homosexuals, who, like the Jews with whom they "were frequently bracketed in medieval persecutions[,] ... are despised more for who they are than for what they do ..."[28] Recall, too, that

> the judge's famous speech at Oscar Wilde's sentencing for sodomy, one of the most prominent legal texts in the history of homosexuality, "treats the prisoners as objects of disgust, vile contaminants who are not really people, and who therefore need not be addressed as if they were people." From this it is not very far to Heinrich Himmler's speech to his SS generals, in which he explained that the medieval German practice of drowning gay men in

[28] Richard Posner, Sex and Reason 346 (1992). Cf. Louis Crompton, Homosexuality and Civilization (2003). Crompton's book is discussed in Edward Rothstein, "Annals of Homosexuality: From Greek to Grim to Gay," New York Times, December 13, 2003.

As history teaches, "an irrational fear and loathing" of *any* group "more for who they are than for what they do" has tragic consequences. The irrational fear and loathing of homosexuals – that is, the fear and loathing of them *more for who they are than for what they do* – is no exception. There is, for example, the horrible phenomenon of "gay bashing." "The coordinator of one hospital's victim assistance program reported that 'attacks against gay men were the most heinous and brutal I encountered.' A physician reported that injuries suffered by the victims of homophobic violence he had treated were so 'vicious' as to make clear that 'the intent is to kill and maim'..." Andrew Koppelman, Antidiscrimination Law & Social Equality 165 (1996). As "[a] federal task force on youth suicide noted[,] because 'gay youth face a hostile and condemning environment, verbal and phyical abuse, and rejection and isolation from family and peers,' young gays are two to three times more likely than other young people to attempt and to commit suicide." Id. at 149.

> bogs "was no punishment, merely the extermination of an abnormal life. It had to be removed just as we [now] pull up stinging nettles, toss them on a heap, and burn them."[29]

We may fairly wonder, however, whether in contemporary liberal democracies, including the United States, the "irrational fear and loathing" to which Judge Posner refers – the view that homosexuals are not truly, fully human – explains much of the opposition to extending the benefit of law to same-sex unions. Indeed, the pope and the bishops of the Catholic Church are among the foremost opponents of extending the benefit of law to same-sex unions; nonetheless, the teaching of the pope and the bishops "about the dignity of homosexual persons is clear. They must be accepted with respect, compassion, and sensitivity. Our respect for them means that we condemn all forms of unjust discrimination, harrassment or abuse."[30] Hate the sin, but love the sinner.[31]

In any event, laws (and other policies) that discriminate against homosexuals – that discriminate against persons, that

[29] Andrew Koppelman, "Are the Boy Scouts Being as Bad as Racists? Judging the Scouts' Antigay Policy," 18 Public Affairs Quarterly 363, 372 (2004).

[30] USCCB Administrative Committee, "Promote, Protect, Preserve Marriage: Statement on Marriage and Homosexual Unions," 33 Origins 257, 259 (2003).

[31] See Robert F. Nagel, "Playing Defense in Colorado," First Things, May 1998, at 34, 35: "There is the obvious but important possibility that one can 'hate' an individual's behavior without hating the individual."

treat them less well, qua homosexuals – are at least superficially different from laws that discriminate against same-sex sexual (*genital*) conduct: Unlike laws of the former sort, which apply just to homosexuals, even if they are celibate, laws of the latter sort apply to persons without regard to whether they are homosexuals. (A law that prevents homosexuals from serving as teachers in a public school system is a law of the former sort.) Do laws of the latter sort – in particular, refusals to extend the benefit of law to same-sex unions – violate the Fourteenth Amendment? Laws of the latter sort treat some citizens – those who engage in same-sex sexual conduct – less well than other citizens – those who do not engage in such conduct. Are such laws based on the view that those treated less well are, because they engage in such conduct, second-class citizens? Or, instead, are they simply efforts to serve the public good? What public good? The public good of not encouraging (incentivizing) conduct – here, sexual conduct – believed to be immoral. "The racism analogy has some power; much of the antigay animus that exists in the United States is just like racism, in the virulence of the rage it bespeaks and the hatred it directs towards those who are its objects."[32] Nonetheless, "[n]ot all antigay views . . . deny

[32] Andrew Koppelman, "You Can't Hurry Love: Why Antidiscrimination Protections for Gay People Should Have Religious Exemptions," 72 Brooklyn L. Rev. 125, 145 (2006).

the personhood and equal citizenship of gay people.... There is a serious discussion to be had here about sexuality and morality."[33]

Most states refuse to recognize – they refuse to extend the benefit of law to – same-sex unions.[34] In so doing, a state

> effectively excludes [same-sex partners] from a broad array of legal benefits and protections incident to the marital relation, including access to a spouse's medical, life, and disability insurance, hosptial visitation and other medical decisionmaking privileges, spousal support, intestate succession, homestead protections, and many other stautory protections.[35]

[33] Id.

[34] See Lewis v. Harris, 908 A.2d at 219: "Today, only Connecticut and Vermont, through civil unions, and Massachusetts, through marriage, extend to committed same-sex couples the full rights and benefits offered to married heterosexual couples.... A few jurisdictions [namely, California, Hawaii, Maine, and the District of Columbia]... offer some but not all of those rights under domestic partnership schemes." Given the New Jersey Supreme Court's decision in *Lewis v. Harris*, and recent legislation in New Hampshire, New Jersey and New Hampshire are now aligned with Connecticut, Massachusetts, and Vermont. According to a 2007 Pew Research Center survey, a majority of Americans (55 percent) opposes legalizing same-sex marriage but a significant minority (37 percent) supports it. Moreover, a majority of Americans (54 percent) supports civil unions for gays and lesbians, according to a 2006 Pew survey.

As of this writing (2008), the Netherlands (since 2000), Belgium (2003), Spain (2005), Canada (2005), and South Africa (2006) have all legalized same-sex marriage.

[35] Baker v. Vermont, 744 A.2d 864, 870 (VT 1999). For a fuller specification of the benefits in question, see id. at 883–84. See also Goodridge v. [Massachusetts] Department of Public Health, 798 N.E.2d 941, 955–57 (MA 2003); Hernandez v. Robles, 855 N.E.2d 1, 6–7 (NY 2006).

Again, a court committed to Thayerian deference should ask whether it is reasonable to conclude that (1) the good the differential treatment aims to serve is a public good, (2) the differential treatment actually serves that good and (3) it does so in a proportionate fashion. But first a court must ascertain what good (or goods) the differential treatment aims to serve.

On July 6, 2006, a majority of the Court of Appeals of the State of New York (New York's highest court) – in an opinion that within weeks was endorsed both by a three-judge panel of the United States Court of Appeals for the Eighth Circuit (July 14, 2006) and by a majority of the Supreme Court of the State of Washington (July 26, 2006) – indicated that the goods New York's refusal to extend the benefit of law to same-sex unions aim to serve are twofold: (1) minimizing the number of children born out of wedlock, and (2) maximizing the number of children raised by their mother and father together.[36] Good (1) and good (2) are undeniably public goods.[37] Even

[36] See Hernandez v. Robles, 855 N.E.2d 1, 7–8 (NY 2006); Citizens for Equal Protection v. Bruning, 455 F.3d 859, 867–68 (8th Cir. 2006); Andersen v. King County, 138 P.3d 963, 982–85 (WA 2006).

[37] Maximizing the number of children raised by two parents is a public good *without regard to whether the two parents are a heterosexual couple or a same-sex couple*. See Lewis v. Harris, 908 A.2d 196, 230 (NJ 2006) (Poritz, C. J., joined by Long & Zazzali, JJ., concurring in part & dissenting in part):

> Recent social science studies inform us that "same-sex couples increasingly form the core of families in which children are conceived, born, and raised. Gregory N. Herek, *Legal Recognition of*

if we assume that extending the benefit of law to heterosexual unions makes it more likely that children will be born in wedlock and raised by their mother and father together, it strains credulity past the breaking point to believe that good (1) and good (2) are the public goods that New York's (or any other state's) policy of extending the benefit of law *just* to heterosexual unions aims to serve. We all know that the benefit of law is extended to heterosexual unions *for a set of related reasons (that is, public goods) that have nothing to do either with minimizing the number of children born out of wedlock or maximizing the number of children raised by their mother and father together*: To protect and nurture (by law) the solemn commitment each person makes to the other to unite their lives in a lifelong, monogamous relationship of mutual love and support; to protect the persons who have made that commitment and are living their lives accordingly; and to protect the children who have been born to or adopted by the couple. Those reasons simply do not explain refusing to extend the benefit of law to same-sex unions; indeed, by themselves

Same-Sex Couples in the United States: A Social Science Perspective, 61 *Am. Psychol.* 607, 611 (2006). It is not surprising, given that data, that the State does not advance a "promotion of procreation" position to support limiting marriage to heterosexuals. Further, "[e]mpirical studies comparing children raised by sexual minority parents with those raised by otherwise comparable heterosexual parents have not found reliable disparities in mental health or social adjustment," id. at 613, suggesting that the "optimal environment" position is equally weak.

those reasons call for the opposite policy. The point is so obvious that elaboration would be otiose: Don't same-sex partners who have made a commitment to one another to unite their lives in a lifelong, monogamous relationship of mutual love and support, and who are living their lives accordingly, need the protection of the law? Don't the children who have been born to or adopted by the same-sex couple need the protection of the law?[38] So, again, what good(s) do state refusals to extend the benefit of law to same-sex unions aim to serve?

Political opposition to legalizing same-sex unions discloses two such goods, the first of which is the (undeniably public) good of protecting heterosexual marriage.

> In the 1990s, the opponents of same-sex marriage created a new line of argument critique. The new line, which

[38] For answers to those and many other relevant questions – answers that lead Professor McClain to support extending the benefit of law to same-sex unions – see Linda C. McClain, The Place of Families: Fostering Capacity, Equality, and Responsibility (2006); Linda C. McClain, "God's Created Order, Gender Complementarity, and the Federal Marriage Amendment," 20 Brigham Young University Journal of Public Law 313 (2006). Cf. The Brussels Declaration, https://www.iheu.org/v4e/html/the_declaration.html.

Modern families come in a wide variety of forms: the traditional nuclear or extended families, single-parent families, unmarried couples with or without children, same-sex couples, even – in some AIDS-stricken societies – children with no parents at all. Whatever form the family may take, the primary responsibility of parents is to safeguard and nurture their children. No child should suffer discrimination because of his or her family circumstances. All are equally entitled to protection and support.

has been embraced within the White House and the most anti-gay circles of Capitol Hill, is this: "We love gays and lesbians – but as a society we cannot give them things that would undermine traditional marriage, which is the foundation of America's values and culture. Same-sex marriage would do precisely that – undermine marriage and the nuclear family. For that reason, neutral people should be skeptical of complete equality for these people.... We traditionalists love just about everyone – and look what we've done for homosexuals, we don't put them in jail anymore. But a positive and loving approach requires that we consider the public welfare, especially the welfare of children, our most vulnerable charges. So we cannot go along with the entire 'homosexual agenda,' for it sacrifices a great institution and the public welfare."[39]

[39] William N. Eskridge Jr., Darren R. Spedale, & Hans Ytterberg, "Nordic Bliss? Scandinavian Registered Partnerships and the Same-Sex Marriage Debate" at 4, Berkeley Electronic Press, Issues in Legal Scholarship, Symposium: Single-Sex Marriage (2004), Article 4, www.bepress.com/ils/iss5/art4.

According to Peter Berkowitz, "conservatives' most important argument" against gay marriage is this: "Given the changes in the social meaning of marriage over the past forty years, conservatives worry that the legalization of same-sex marriage will further attenuate the connection between marriage and family that is crucial to a healthy society." Peter Berkowitz, "Illiberal Liberalism," First Things, April 2007, at 50, 54. However, Berkowitz doesn't tell us how, and it is far from obvious that, "the legalization of same-sex marriage will further attenuate the connection between marriage and family that is crucial to a healthy society." Maybe the argument he has in mind is the argument pressed by the pope and the bishops of the Catholic Church. See n. 47 and accompanying text.

Is it plausible to think – as the pope and bishops of the Catholic Church, among others, do – that extending the benefit of law to same-sex unions would have, in the long run, subversive consequences for heterosexual marriage?[40] Because that claim is both bereft of empirical support[41] and, for many, deeply counterintuitive,[42] many reject the claim as implausible. It is not surprising that the New York and Washington justices referenced two paragraphs ago, determined as they conspicuously were to lob the controversy over same-sex unions

[40] See Stephen J. Pope, "The Magisterium's Arguments against 'Same-Sex Marriage': An Ethical Analysis and Critique," 65 Theological Studies 530, 559 (2004) (citing Judith S. Wallerstein & Sandra Blakeless, The Good Marriage: How and Why Love Lasts (1995)):

> The magisterium [i.e., the pope and the bishops] fears that a purely non-procreative, contractualized notion of marriage might lead to the elimination of the family and to anarchy in child-rearing practices. They believe that even conservative gays who want to have the monogamous commitments receive the social support that comes from legal validation are, unwittingly or not, pursuing a Trojan horse policy in which entry into the institution will eventually lead to its demise. Instead of helping matters, contractualism would leave them on their own and make it easier for fathers routinely to abandon their children.

Cf. Geoffrey Nunberg, "We the People? (In Order to Form a More Perfect Gay Union)," New York Times, February 22, 2004: "For opponents [of recognizing same-sex unions as marriages], broadening the definition of marriage is like opening an exclusive hotel to package tours, with the result that the traditional clientele will no longer feel like checking in."

[41] See William N. Eskridge Jr. & Darren R. Spedale, Gay Marriage: For Better or Worse?: What We've Learned from the Evidence (2006).

[42] See, for example, Jonathan Rauch, "Family's Value: Gay Marriage is Good for Kids," New Republic, May 30, 2005, at 15; Rosemary Radford Ruether, "Marriage Between Homosexuals Is Good for Marriage," National Catholic Reporter, November 18, 2005, at 20.

back into the laps of the state legislators,[43] did not rely on the putative plausibility of the claim to buttress their ruling.[44]

[43] See Hernandez v. Robles, 855 N.E.2d 1, 22 (NY 2006); Andersen v. King County, 138 P.3d 963, 990 (WA 2006).

[44] A different reason for refusing to extend the benefit of law to same-sex unions has been mounted by British philosopher Roger Scruton. Here is Scruton's argument, as summarized by Roderick Hills:

> [O]ne might reasonably believe that men and women have different and complementary sexual "temperaments" such that sexual relationships between members of different sexes will be more psychologically satisfactory than relationships between members of the same sex. Scruton argues that men tend to be more sexually predatory and promiscuous than women; while women seek permanence in their sexual relationships, men tend to seek adventure. Therefore, if men form sexual relationships with other men rather than with women, those relationships will tend to have shorter duration and a greater concentration on physical self-gratification than heterosexual relationships. If one assumes that these characteristics are undesirable, then one might conclude that at least male homosexuality is undesirable.

Roderick M. Hills Jr., "You Say You Want a Revolution? The Case Against the Transformation of Culture Through Nondiscrimination Laws," 95 Michigan L. Rev. 1588, 1610–11 (1997) (citing Roger Scruton, Sexual Desire: A Moral Philosophy of the Erotic 305–11 (1986)).

It is doubtful that we should credit Scruton's controversial generalizations. See Martha C. Nussbaum, "Platonic Love and Colorado Law: The Relevance of Ancient Greek Norms to Modern Sexual Controversies," 80 Virginia L. Rev. 1515, 1601 (1994):

> Scruton's argument was always a peculiar one: for why should one believe that all individuals of one sex are more like each other in quality than any of them is like any member of the opposite sex? And would Scruton really wish to generalize his argument, as consistency seems to demand, preferring relationships between partners different in age, and race, and nationality, and religion? Even if he were to do so, Plato's dialogues offer good argument against him. Along with Aristotle's ethical thought, they argue that people who are alike in the goals they share and the aspirations they cherish may be more likely to promote genuine social goods than people who are unlike in character and who do not share any aspirations. In addition, the dialogues show that the kind

So let's cut to the chase. There is a second good that state refusals to extend to benefit of law to same sex unions aim to serve, and it has nothing to do with protecting heterosexual marriage – or with minimizing the number of children born

> of "otherness" that is valuable in love relationships – that one's partner is another separate and, to some extent, hidden world; that the body shows only traces of the soul within; and that lovers never can be completely welded together into a single person – is quite different from the "qualitative" otherness of physiology and character. Indeed, the "otherness" of mystery and separateness is actually defended in Scruton's argument, as it is in Plato's, as an erotic good.

But even if, for the sake of discussion, we credit his generalizations, Scruton's argument fails as an argument against extending the benefit of law to same-sex unions. First, the argument doesn't explain why government should refuse to recognize woman–woman unions. Second, the argument doesn't explain why, even if in general man–woman unions might be "more psychologically satisfactory" than man–man unions, government should refuse to recognize man–man unions if those who form such unions are incapable of forming man–woman unions. Third, the argument doesn't explain why, even if in general man–man sexual relationships are more transitory than man–woman sexual relationships, government should refuse to recognize the man–man sexual relationships of those who are committed to, and seek public affirmation of, their relationships as *lifelong unions of faithful love*. There is no reason to think that legal recognition of such relationships would do the relationships harm – and no reason to doubt that legal recognition would do the relationships good. See Andrew Sullivan, "Three's a Crowd," New Republic, June 17, 1996, at 10, 12:

> [M]arriage acts both as an incentive for virtuous behavior – and as a social blessing for the effort. In the past, we have wisely not made nitpicking assessments as to who deserves the right to marry and who does not. We have provided it to anyone prepared to embrace it and hoped for the best.... For some, it comes easily. For others, its responsibilities and commitments are crippling. But we do not premise the right to marry upon the ability to perform its demands flawlessly. We accept that human beings are variably virtuous, but that, as citizens, they should be given the same rights and responsibilities – period.

out of wedlock or maximizing the number of children raised by their mother and father together:

- Government should not adopt policies – it is a public good for government to refrain from adopting policies – that encourage (incentivize) immoral conduct.
- To extend the benefit of law to same-sex unions would be to encourage same-sex sexual conduct.
- Same-sex sexual conduct is immoral.

Therefore, government should not extend the benefit of law to same-sex unions.[45]

Let's assume, for the sake of discussion, both that it is a public good for government to refrain from adopting policies that encourage immoral conduct and that to extend the benefit of law to same-sex unions would be to encourage same-sex sexual conduct. If no argument in support of the view that same-sex sexual conduct is immoral is plausible, then one

See also David Brooks, "The Power of Marriage," New York Times, November 22, 2003.

Andrew Koppelman has argued that "even in the present regime in which they are not permitted to marry, same-sex couples do not seem to be much less stable than heterosexual couples. [The] data suggests that same-sex couples are not all that different in terms of their capacity to function or to remain stable from heterosexual couples." Koppelman, "Three Arguments for Gay Rights," 95 Michigan L. Rev. 1636, 1666. See id. at 1664–66.

45 See Andersen v. King County, 138 P.3d 963, 980 (WA 2006) (majority opinion); id. at 1032 et seq. (dissenting op'n).

cannot reasonably conclude that refusing to extend the benefit of law to same-sex unions serves the public good of not encouraging immoral conduct. So, is there a plausible argument in support of the view that same-sex sexual conduct is immoral?

Again, among the foremost critics of proposals to extend the benefit of law to same-sex unions are the pope and the bishops of the Catholic Church, who "[strongly oppose] any legislative and judicial attempts, both at state and federal levels, to grant same-sex unions the equivalent status and rights of marriage – by naming them marriage, civil unions or by other means."[46] As it happens, when the pope or the bishops are in the public square (so to speak) to weigh in on political controversies, they rely on *non-religious* arguments: arguments that presuppose the authority neither of Christianity (much less of Catholicism) nor, indeed, of any religious belief. The principal secular argument on the basis of which the Church opposes the legal recognition of same-sex unions holds that it is immoral for anyone to engage, voluntarily and intentionally, in any species of sex (genital) act that of its nature ("inherently") is not procreative – masturbation, for example; or male-female sexual intercourse, even in marriage, in which the man uses a condom; or oral copulation.

[46] USCCB Administrative Committee, n. 30, at 259.

According to the Administrative Committee of the U.S. Conference of Catholic Bishops, "[w]hat are called 'homosexual unions,'... *because they are inherently nonprocreative*, cannot be given the status of marriage."[47]

Is the Church's secular argument plausible?[48] Happily, we don't have to enter that thicket: For most citizens of the United States, the Church's argument about the immorality of inherently non-procreative sex – about, for example, the immorality of marital intercourse in which the husband uses a condom – is not plausible; indeed, the argument is not plausible even for most American *Catholics*. (If the argument were plausible for most American Catholics, presumably many more American Catholics would practice what their Church preaches. But in fact relatively few do.)[49] Hence the Church's secular argument

[47] Id. (emphasis added).

[48] For a recent elaboration of the Church's argument against the legal recognition of same-sex marriage, see Robert P. George, "Law and Moral Purpose," First Things, January 2008, at 22, 25–28.

[49] Even for one who accepts the Church's argument, it does not follow that *none* of the benefits of law should be extended to same-sex unions. Significantly, some Catholic bishops in the United States have recently expressed a willingness to consider supporting, as a matter of distributive justice, the extension of *some* of the benefits of law to same-sex unions. See Editorial, "Bishop Brings Reason to Issue of Gay Benefits," National Catholic Rptr., November 7, 2003, at 24:

> [Daniel P.] Reilly[, Roman Catholic bishop of Worcester, Massachusetts,] told legislators that the Massachusetts Catholic Conference, made up of the dioceses of Boston, Worcester, Springfield, and Fall River, was unequivocally opposed to legislation that would recognize gay "marriage" or "civil unions." But the church is open, he said, to discussing what public benefits should accrue

in support of the view that same-sex sexual conduct is (per se) immoral does not explain, it does not underlie, say, the State

> to those in non-traditional relationships. . . . "If the goal is to look at individual benefits and determine who should be eligible beyond spouses, then we will join the discussion," said Reilly. . . . [Reilly] engaged the issue on the church's terms, saying such benefits are a matter of "distributive justice." . . .
>
> "Some argue that it is unfair to offer only married couples certain socioeconomic benefits," Reilly told [a committee of Massachusetts legislators]. "That is a different question from the meaning of marriage itself. The civil union bill before this committee confuses the two issues, changing the meaning of spouse in order to give global access to all marital benefits to same-sex partners in a civil union. This alters the institution of marriage by expanding whom the law considers to be spouses. Let's not mix the two issues."

More recently, the papal nuncio to Spain, Archbishop Manuel Monteiro de Castro, "has surprised public opinion by defending legal same-sex unions as a 'right.'" See "Nuncio Backs 'Right' to Gay Unions," The Tablet [London], May 15, 2004, at 30: "The nuncio's words took commentators by surprise, as the Spanish bishops officially hold the view that homosexual relationships cannot receive any kind of approval. . . . 'It is right that other types of relationship are recognised,' the nuncio said. He added that those in such unions should have the same rights to social security 'as any other citizen.' But 'let's leave the term "marriage" for that to which it has always referred,' he added." See also "Sign of the Times," America, November 15, 2004, at 4, 5:

> Bishop George H. Niederauer of Salt Lake City did not endorse the proposed constitutional amendment in Utah, saying that he believed that state law already prohibited same-sex marriages. He said he shared concerns voiced by all three candidates for attorney general about the amendment's stipulation that "no other domestic union may be recognized as a marriage given the same or substantially equal legal effect."

Cf. Jennifer 8. Lee, "Congressman Says Bush Is Open to States' Bolstering Gay Rights," New York Times, February 9, 2004 ("President Bush believes states can use contract law to ensure some of the rights that gay partners are seeking through marriage or civil union, a South

of Georgia's refusal to extend the benefit of law to same-sex unions.[50]

Carolina congressman said Sunday."); Brian Lavery, "Ireland: Premier Backs Rights for Gay Couples," New York Times, November 16, 2004 ("Prime Minister Bertie Ahern said his government might consider giving same-sex couples more rights, which would allow them to benefit from cheaper tax rates and more favorable inheritance laws.").

50 For anyone who rejects the Church's argument about the immorality of inherently non-procreative sex,

> it is no longer possible to argue that sex/love between two persons of the same sex cannot be a valid embrace of bodily selves expressing love. If sex/love is centered primarily on communion between two selves *rather than on biologistic concepts of procreative complementarity*, then the love of two persons of the same sex need be no less than that of two persons of the opposite sex. Nor need their experience of ecstatic bodily communion be less valuable.

Rosemary Ruether, "The Personalization of Sexuality," in Eugene Bianchi & Rosemary Ruether, eds., From Machismo to Mutuality: Essays on Sexism and Woman-Man Liberation 70, 83 (1976) (emphasis added). Cf. Edward Collins Vacek, SJ, "The Meaning of Marriage: Of Two Minds," Commonweal, October 24, 2003, at 17, 18–19: "When, after Vatican II, Catholics began to connect sexual activity more strongly with expressing love than with making babies, it became harder to see how homosexual acts are completely different from heterosexual acts." However, to conclude that same-sex sexual conduct is not inherently immoral does not entail that anything goes. As Margaret Farley, a Catholic sister and Stark Professor of Christian Ethics at Yale University, has written:

> My answer [to the question of what norms should govern same-sex relations and activities] has been: the norms of justice – the norms which govern all human relationships and those which are particular to the intimacy of sexual relations. Most generally, the norms are respect for persons through respect for autonomy and rationality; respect for relationality through requirements of mutuality, equality, commitment, and fruitfulness. More specifically one might say things like: sex between two persons of the same sex (just as two persons of the opposite sex) should not be used in a way that exploits, objectifies, or dominates; homosexual (like heterosexual) rape, violence, or any harmful use of power against unwilling victims (or those incapacitated by reason of age,

The argument that *does* underlie such refusals – the argument in support of the view that same-sex sexual conduct is immoral – is not secular but religious: "According to the Bible, which discloses to us the will of God, same-sex unions are contrary to the will of God." For many citizens of the United States – including many who self-identify as Christian, even as evangelical Christian – a biblically based argument that same-sex unions are contrary to the will of God is simply not credible.[51] Many other Americans, however, affirm one or another version of just that argument. It is utterly unrealistic to expect the Supreme Court to pass judgment on the

> etc.) is never justified; freedom, integrity, privacy are values to be affirmed in every homosexual (as heterosexual) relationship; all in all, individuals are not to be harmed, and the common good is to be promoted.

Margaret A. Farley, "An Ethic for Same-Sex Relations," in Robert Nugent, ed., A Challenge to Love: Gay and Lesbian Catholics in the Church 93, 105 (1983). Farley then adds that "[t]he Christian community will want and need to add those norms of faithfulness, forgiveness, of patience and hope, which are essential to any relationships between persons in the Church." Id. See also Margaret Farley, Just Love: A Framework for Christian Sexual Ethics (2006).

51 See, for example, David G. Meyers & Letha Dawson Scanzoni, What God Has Joined Together? A Christian Case for Gay Marriage (2005). I have explained elsewhere why Christians, *as Christians*, have good reason to be wary about relying on this biblically based argument as a ground for opposing the legal recognition of same-sex unions. See Michael J. Perry, Under God? Religious Faith and Liberal Democracy 55–80 (2003). Cf. Nicholas D. Kristof, "Lovers Under the Skin," New York Times, December 3, 2003: "A 1958 poll found that 96 percent of whites disapproved of marriages between blacks and whites.... In 1959 a judge justified Virginia's ban on interracial marriage by declaring that 'Almighty God... did not intend for the races to mix.'"

plausibility of religious arguments, least of all religious arguments that so many Americans affirm.[52] Fortunately, the Court need not even contemplate doing so, because the constitutional imperative that government not establish religion, properly understood, bans sectarian religious arguments as a basis of lawmaking. (I defend that proposition in the postscript to this book.)[53] And the argument that same-sex sexual conduct is contrary to the will of God is undeniably sectarian. Indeed, the argument is sectarian even among Christians: That same-sex sexual conduct is contrary to the will of God is contested among Christians; although accepted by many Christians, the claim is rejected – increasingly so – by many Christians.[54] The claim is also contested among

[52] Cf. "Gay Marriage–Posner's Response to Comments," The Becker–Posner Blog, July 24, 2005, http://becker-posner-blog.com: "I think the main basis for the opposition [to gay marriage] is religious and . . . that such opposition is different from opposition based on a scientific error. Religion is not scientific, but there is a difference between a belief that is demonstrably based on error and a belief based on a system of thought that science neither supports nor refutes."

[53] As I explain in the postscript, "sectarian religious" argument is not redundant: There are some religious arguments that are not sectarian for purposes of the non-establishment norm.

[54] See Brian K. Blount, "Reading and Understanding the New Testament on Homosexuality," Homosexuality and Christian Community; Victor Paul Furnish, "The Bible and Homosexuality: Reading the Texts in Context," Homosexuality in the Church; Daniel A. Helminiak, "The Bible on Homosexuality: Ethically Neutral," Same Sex; Patricia Beattie Jung & Ralph F. Smith, "The Bible and Heterosexism," Patricia Beattie Jung & Ralph F. Smith, Heterosexism: An Ethical Challenge 61 (1993); Bruce J. Malina, "The New Testament and Homosexuality," in Patricia Beattie Jung, with Joseph Andrew Coray, eds., Sexual Diversity and Catholicism: Toward the Development of Moral Theology

religious Jews; some Jewish congregations bless same-sex unions. And the claim is beginning to be contested even among Muslims.[55] So under the non-establishment norm, the rationale that same-sex sexual conduct is contrary to the will of God is not a legitimate basis of lawmaking.

Again, is there an argument – other than the "contrary to the will of God" argument – in support of the view that same-sex sexual conduct is immoral? As I have explained in this chapter, I can discern none. So I conclude that state refusals to extend the benefit of law to same-sex unions violate the Fourteenth Amendment. More precisely, they violate the Fourteenth Amendment's mandate of equal citizenship *when that mandate is read, as of course it must be, in conjunction with an imperative the Fourteenth Amendment makes applicable to the states, namely, that government not establish religion.*[56]

150 (2001); Choon-Leong Seow, "A Heterotextual Perspective," Homosexuality and Christian Community; Jeffrey S. Siker, "Homosexual Christians, the Bible, and Gentile Inclusion: Confessions of a Repenting Heterosexist," Homosexuality in the Church.

55 See, for example, Arash Naraghi, "Islam and the Moral Status of Homosexuality":

http://www.uweb.ucsb.edu/~anaraghi/articles/Islamandminorities.pdf

56 The First Amendment to the United States Constitution states: "Congress shall make no law respecting an establishment of religion, or prohibiting the free exercise thereof..." I concur in Kent Greenawalt's judgment that "[b]y far the most plausible reading of the original religion clauses – based on their text, the history leading up to their enactment, and legislation enacted by Congress – is that Congress could protect but not impair free exercise in carrying out its delegated powers for the entire country and within exclusively federal domains, that Congress could neither establish a religion within the states nor

Indeed, I also conclude that even a Supreme Court committed to Thayerian deference could rule that state refusals to extend the benefit of law to same-sex unions violate the Fourteenth Amendment: A Thayerian justice could conclude, as I have in this chapter, that the claim that such refusals serve the public good is not only mistaken but unreasonable.

Let's now cross the line that separates the domain of constitutional law from the murky realm of constitutional politics. Assume for the sake of discussion that at the present time (2008), a majority of the justices of the United States Supreme Court agree that state refusals to extend the benefit

interfere with state establishments [of religion], and that Congress could not establish religion within exclusively federal domains." Kent Greenawalt, "Common Sense about Original and Subsequent Understandings of the Religion Clauses," 8 J. Constitutional Law 479, 511 (2005). See also id. at 491.

The religion clauses have long been held to apply – it is constitutional bedrock that they apply – not just to Congress but to the entire national government, and not just to the national government but to state government as well. In effect, then, the clauses provide that government may neither establish religion nor prohibit the free exercise thereof. See Michael W. McConnell, "Accommodation of Religion: An Update and Response to the Critics," 60 George Washington L. Rev. 685, 690 (1992): "The government may not 'establish' religion and it may not 'prohibit' religion." McConnell explains, in a footnote attached to the word "establish," that "[t]he text [of the First Amendment] states the 'Congress' may make no law 'respecting an establishment' of religion, which meant that Congress could neither establish a national church nor interfere with the establishment of state churches as they then existed in the various states. After the last disestablishment in 1833 and the incorporation of the First Amendment against the states through the Fourteenth Amendment, this 'federalism' aspect of the Amendment has lost its significance, and the Clause can be read as forbidding the government to establish religion." Id. at 690 n. 19.

of law to same-sex unions violate the Fourteenth Amendment. Would it make good political sense for the Court, at this time, to so rule? Many who want states to extend the benefit of law to same-sex unions worry that it would be counterproductive for the Court to rule that states must do so. Perhaps it would be counterproductive – even greatly counterproductive – for the Court to so rule; if so, perhaps it would be best, all things considered, for the Court to do what it can to avoid ruling on the question at all.[57]

[57] Cf. Alexander M. Bickel, The Least Dangerous Branch: The Supreme Court at the Bar of Politics 111–98 (1962); Gerald Gunther, "The Subtle Vices of the 'Passive Virtues': A Comment on Principle and Expediency in Judicial Review," 64 Columbia L. Rev. 1 (1964).

Assume, however, that the Court cannot avoid ruling on the question. Should the Court, in ruling, pretend that it finds plausible that which many others find implausible and which the Court itself, in other, changed political circumstances, would find implausible? Commenting on the New York Court of Appeals' decision, on July 6, 2006, in *Hernandez v. Robles*, 855 N.E.2d 1, Peter Beinart, in *The New Republic*, wrote:

> Last week, the New York Court of Appeals handed down a lousy decision on gay marriage. And thank goodness it did. By refusing – on flimsy grounds – to strike down the Empire State's gay marriage ban, the court actually did the gay marriage movement a favor. Gay marriage is coming in America – through the democratic process. If the courts step in, they will only set the effort back. . . . With its shoddy reasoning, the New York Court of Appeals last week helped the gay marriage struggle in the best way it could – it got out of the way.

Peter Beinart, "Judge Knot," New Republic, July 24, 2006, at 6.

Notwithstanding Beinart's comment, whether as a political matter a *state* supreme court should interpret the state constitution to require the state to extend the benefit of law to same-sex unions is a more complicated question than whether as a political matter the United States

(*Footnote 57 continued*)

Supreme Court should interpret the United States Constitution – the Fourteenth Amendment – to require states to extend the benefit of law to same-sex unions. Consider, for example, something Richard Posner has written: Although Posner finds the "argument for recognizing homosexual marriage quite persuasive," he nonetheless thinks that the Supreme Court should not require states to extend the benefit of law to same-sex unions: Such "a radical social policy... is deeply offensive to the vast majority of its citizens.... [For the Court to do so] would be an unprecedented example of judicial immodesty." Posner, "Should There Be Homosexual Marriage," n. 2, at 1584–85. Posner's preference is for "[letting] a state legislature or an activist (but elected, and hence democratically responsive) state court adopt homosexual marriage as a policy in one state, and let the rest of the country learn from the results of its experiment. That is the democratic way..." Id. at 1585–86. As of this writing (2008), the state supreme courts of Vermont, Massachusetts, and New Jersey have interpreted their state constitutions to require their states to extend the benefit of law to same-sex unions – and in none of those states does a "backlash" seem likely. Cf. Carlos A. Ball, "The Backlash Thesis and Same-Sex Marriage: Learning from *Brown v. Board of Education* and Its Aftermath," 14 Wm & Mary Bill of Rights J. 1493 (2006).

CHAPTER FIVE

Abortion

In 1973, in *Roe v. Wade*[1] and *Doe v. Bolton*,[2] the Supreme Court of the United States famously – some would say notoriously – ruled that state laws that ban pre-viability[3] abortions violate the Fourteenth Amendment. Was the Court's ruling, which still stands,[4] correct?[5] In particular, do state bans

[1] 410 U.S. 113.

[2] 410 U.S. 179.

[3] The Supreme Court prefers "previability." See Gonzales v. Carhart, 127 S. Ct. 1610 (2007). I prefer "pre-viability."

[4] In *Planned Parenthood of Southeastern Pennsylvania v. Casey*, 505 U.S. 833 (1992), the Court declined to overrule Roe and Doe. Cf. Gonzales v. Carhart, 127 S. Ct. 1610 (2007) (Partial-Birth Abortion Ban Act of 2003 is not unconstitutional).

[5] Cf. Michael W. McConnell, "Active Liberty: A Progressive Alternative to Textualism and Originalism?," 119 Harvard L. Rev. 2387, 2401 (2006) (reviewing Stephen Breyer, Active Liberty: Interpreting Our Democratic Constitution (2006)):

> What about the dog that didn't bark? No theory of interpretation today is complete without some discussion of *Roe v. Wade*,

on pre-viability abortions violate any part of the second sentence of Section 1 of the Fourteenth Amendment? Although such bans don't implicate, much less violate, either the due process clause or the equal protection clause (that is, given the original understanding of the clauses), they do implicate the privileges or immunities clause – as does any law that treats some citizens less well than other citizens.[6] (I can't think of a regulatory law that doesn't treat some citizens less well than others.)[7] A ban on pre-viability abortions – although it applies to everyone and not just, say, to African Americans – treats some citizens less well than others: It treats those who have had a pre-viability abortion (or who have performed one)[8] less well than those who have not by punishing those who have had a pre-viability abortion.

But to implicate is not necessarily to violate. Recall from the preceding chapter that according to the Fourteenth

abortion, and substantive due process. Yet these words do not so much as appear in Justice Breyer's book. For many informed people, even many supporters of abortion rights, the Supreme Court's decision in *Roe v. Wade* is the *über*-example, the 800-pound gorilla, of unrestrained judging.

[6] See Chapter 4, nn. 4–26 and accompanying text.

[7] See Michael J. Perry, We the People: The Fourteenth Amendment and the Supreme Court 153–54 (1999).

[8] Cf. M. Cathleen Kaveny, "Toward a Thomistic Perspective on Abortion and the Law in Contemporary America," 55 The Thomist 343, 393 (1991): "[C]riminal sanctions . . . should be directed primarily at physicians rather than women, who are likely to be obtaining even the most morally dubious abortions under conditions of duress."

Amendment, a state may not discriminate against any of its citizens – it may not treat any of its citizens less well than any of its other citizens – on the basis of the view that they are second-class citizens. Recall too that sometimes it is obvious that a law that treats some citizens (non-whites, women, and so on) less well than others is based on the view that those treated less well are second-class citizens. And when it is obvious, the case is at an end: A state may not treat any of its citizens as second-class. Sometimes, however, it is not obvious, and when it is not obvious, a court must bring to bear the requirement that a state may not treat any of its citizens less well *except pursuant to an exercise of the state's "police" power*: the state's legislative power to serve (protect, secure) the public good. No law – no instance of differential treatment – is an exercise of the police power unless three conditions are satisfied:

1. The good the differential treatment aims to serve is a *public* good: a good implicating what modern human rights instruments call "the public safety, the public order, the public health, the public morals, or the fundamental rights and freedoms of others."[9]
2. The differential treatment actually serves the good it aims to serve.

[9] See Chapter 4, n. 7.

3. The differential treatment serves the good it aims to serve in a proportionate fashion: The costs the law imposes on those it treats less well are not so great, so disproportionate, relative to the good the law serves that there is no reasonable justification – no reasonable case to be made – for the differential treatment.[10]

From a Thayerian perspective, the question for a court is not whether in its own judgment the three conditions are satisfied but only whether the claim that the conditions are satisfied is reasonable. A court committed to Thayerian deference should ask whether it is reasonable to conclude that (1) the good the differential treatment aims to serve is a public good, (2) the differential treatment actually serves that good, and (3) it does so in a proportionate fashion. (Recall from Chapter 2 that a conclusion is reasonable if rational, well-informed, and thoughtful persons could reach the conclusion.) If it is unreasonable to regard the good the differential treatment aims to serve as a genuinely public good or to think that the differential treatment serves that good in a proportionate fashion, then the default conclusion is that the differential treatment is based on the view that those treated less well are second-class citizens.

[10] See Perry, We the People, n. 7, at 57–77. What about "incorporation" of the Bill of Rights? To oversimplify, a state law is not a reasonable exercise of the police power if the law, were it a national (federal) law, would violate the Bill of Rights. See id. at 77–80.

Does a ban on pre-viability abortions violate the mandate of equal citizenship? I have suggested elsewhere[11] that:

> 1. The answer is yes if the ban is based on – if it would not have been enacted but for – sex-selective sympathy and indifference, because in that case the ban would affirm that women are second-class citizens – in particular, that their interests matter less than the interests of men.
> 2. One could plausibly conclude that a ban on pre-viability abortions is based on sex-selective sympathy and indifference if the ban did not exempt certain abortions:
>   a. abortions necessary to protect the life of the mother or to protect her physical health from a serious threat of grave and irreparable damage;
>   b. abortions to terminate a pregnancy that began with rape or incest;
>   c. abortions to terminate a pregnancy that because of a grave defect would end with a child "born into what is certain to be a brief life of grievous suffering…"[12]

In the 1973 abortion cases (*Roe* and *Doe*), however, the Supreme Court ruled that any ban on pre-viability abortions – *and, therefore, even a ban that exempts the aforementioned*

[11] See Perry, We the People, n. 7, at 160–66.

[12] John Schwartz, "When Torment is Baby's Destiny, Euthanasia Is Defended," New York Times, March 10, 2005. Cf. Associated Press, "Study: Newborn Euthanasia Often Unreported," New York Times, March 10, 2005.

abortions – violates the Fourteenth Amendment.[13] Assuming for the sake of discussion the authority of the Thayerian perspective, was the Court correct? Is it unreasonable either to regard the good the differential treatment aims to serve as a genuinely public good or to conclude that the differential treatment serves that good in a proportionate fashion?

13 More precisely, the Court ruled that because such bans are not necessary to serve a compelling government purpose, they violate the right of privacy, a right the Court has interpolated from the due process clause of the Fourteenth Amendment. See Roe v. Wade, 410 U.S. 113 (1973).

In the companion case to *Roe* – *Doe v. Bolton*, 410 U.S. 179 (1973) – the Supreme Court invalidated a modern Georgia abortion statute that, while restrictive, was nonetheless more moderate than the much older Texas legislation invalidated in Roe. As the Court put it in *Roe*:

> The Texas statutes under attack here are typical of those that have been in effect in many States for approximately a century. The Georgia statutes, in contrast, have a modern cast and are a legislative product that . . . obviously reflects the influences of recent attitudinal change, of advancing medical knowledge and techniques, and of new thinking about an old issue.

410 U.S. at 116.

The Texas legislation exempted only one category of abortion: abortion "for the purpose of saving the life of the mother." Id. at 118. The Georgia statute, by contrast – which was enacted in 1968 and "patterned upon the American Law Institute's Model Penal Code" (Doe v. Bolton, 410 U.S. at 182) – exempted three categories: "(1) [a] continuation of the pregnancy would endanger the life of the pregnant woman or would seriously and permanently injure her health; or (2) [t]he fetus would very likely be born with a grave, permanent, and irremediable mental or physical defect; or (3) [t]he pregnancy resulted from forcible or statutory rape." Id. at 183. The Court was "assured by [Georgia] at reargument that . . . the statute's reference to 'rape' was intended to include incest." Id. at 183 n. 5.

I. Is it unreasonable to regard the good that bans on pre viability abortions aim to serve as a genuinely public good?

We can imagine laws about which one can sensibly wonder whether the good they aim to serve is a genuinely *public* good. (Consider, for example, a law that forbids married couples to use contraceptives.)[14] However, a law that bans the intentional destruction of a human life is not such a law: The good that such laws – laws against intentional homicide – aim to serve is a genuinely public good.

But is a law that bans pre-viability abortions a law against intentional homicide: Does such a law ban the intentional destruction of a human life? Although, as H. Tristram Engelhardt has observed, "many describe the status of the embryo imprecisely by asking when human life begins or whether the embryo is a human being... no one seriously denies that the human zygote is a human life. The zygote is not dead. It is also not simian, porcine, or canine."[15] Philosopher Peter Singer, who is famously and enthusiatically pro-choice, has acknowledged that "the early embryo is a 'human

[14] See Griswold v. Connecticut, 381 U.S. 479 (1965).

[15] H. Tristram Engelhardt Jr., "Moral Knowledge: Some Reflections on Moral Controversies, Incompatible Moral Epistemologies, and the Culture Wars," 10 Christian Bioethics 79, 84 (2004).

life.' Embryos formed from the sperm and eggs of human beings are certainly human, no matter how early in their development they may be. They are of the species *Homo sapiens*, and not of any other species. We can tell when they are alive, and when they have died. So long as they are alive, they are human life."[16] Similarly, constitutional scholar Laurence Tribe, a staunch pro-choice advocate, has written that "the fetus is alive. It belongs to the human species. It elicits sympathy and even love, in part because it is so dependent and helpless."[17] So a law that bans pre-viability abortions is a law against intentional homicide.

Or is it? One might be tempted to say that a law that bans pre-viability abortions is not a law against intentional homicide *in the relevant sense*: a law that bans the intentional destruction of a human life that has *full moral status*. Even if we accept *arguendo* this characterization of laws against intentional homicide, one can reasonably conclude – as I am about to explain – that every unborn human being has full moral status from the earliest stage of its development; therefore, one can reasonably conclude that a law that bans pre-viability abortions is a law against intentional homicide

[16] Peter Singer, The President of Good and Evil: The Ethics of George W. Bush 37 (2004).

[17] Laurence H. Tribe, "Will the Abortion Fight Ever End: A Nation Held Hostage," New York Times, July 2, 1990, at A13.

in the relevant sense – and, as such, serves the public good.

As it has emerged in the international law of human rights in the period since the end of World War II, the morality of human rights does not hold (though it does not deny either) that every human being has inherent dignity but only that every *born* human being has it. At the beginning of the human rights era, Article 1 of the Universal Declaration of Human Rights (1948) affirmed that "[a]ll human beings are *born* free and equal in dignity and rights" (emphasis added). More than forty years later – well after abortion had emerged as an issue on the political–legal agenda of many liberal democracies, including the United States – the drafters of the international Convention on the Rights of the Child, which entered into force in 1990,[18] specifically declined to use language that would have required state parties to the Convention to ban abortion.[19] So, whereas important international human rights documents – the International Covenant on Civil and Political Rights and the European Convention for the Protection

[18] As of June 2004, there were 192 state parties to the Convention on the Rights of the Child. The United States, which has signed but not ratified the Convention, was not one of them.

[19] See Cynthia Price Cohen, "United Nations Convention on the Rights of the Child: Introductory Note," 44 International Commission of Jurists Rev. 36, 39 (1990); Dominic McGoldrick, "The United Nations Convention on the Rights of the Child," 5 International J. L. & Family 132, 133–34 (1991).

of Human Rights and Fundamental Freedoms – now speak loudly and clearly on the issue of capital punishment,[20] the international law of human rights remains silent on the issue of abortion.[21]

However, that the morality of human rights does not hold that every human being, unborn as well as born, has inherent dignity does not mean that we who affirm the morality of human rights should not do so. Should we who affirm the morality of human rights also affirm that *all* unborn human beings have inherent dignity? or that only *some* unborn human beings have it, namely, those that have reached a certain stage of fetal development? or that *no* unborn human beings have inherent dignity?

[20] See Michael J. Perry, Toward a Theory of Human Rights: Religion, Law, Courts 37–39 (2007).

[21] Cf. Case of Vo v. France, European Court of Human Rights, Application no. 53924/00, July 8, 2004 (Article 2 of the European Convention on Human Rights and Fundamental Freedoms, which states that "[e]veryone's right to life shall be protected by law," does not apply to an "unborn child").

Note, however, that the American Convention on Human Rights states, in Article 1(2), that "[f]or the purposes of this Convention, 'person' means *every* human being"; it then states, in Article 4(1), that "[e]very person has the right to have his life respected" and that "[t]his right shall be protected by law *and, in general, from the moment of conception*." (Emphasis added.) As of April 2005, the American Convention on Human Rights, which entered into force in 1978, had 25 state parties. The United States was not one of them.

It merits mention that the international law of human rights does not remain silent on the issue of reproductive health. See Rebecca J. Cook & Bernard M. Dickens, "Human Rights Dynamics of Abortion Law Reform," 25 Human Rights Quarterly 1 (2003).

What sense would it make to affirm that all *born* human beings have inherent dignity but that no *unborn* human beings have it? Some babies are born after a gestation period of nine months; some are born after a shorter gestation period. (Some babies are born after a shorter gestation period because they are removed from their mother's womb prematurely in order to protect the baby and/or its mother.) It seems quite arbitrary to hold that although a baby born, say, seven months after fertilization acquired inherent dignity the moment it was born, an eight-month-old fetus, because it has not yet been born, has not yet acquired inherent dignity. We who affirm that every born human being has inherent dignity do not all agree about why – in virtue of what – every human being has inherent dignity; we don't all agree about the ground of the inherent dignity we believe every human being to have.[22] But whatever the ground, it seems fair to say that the acquisition of inherent dignity does not depend on the happenstance of whether or not one *has been* born if one *could be* born – that is, born as a *viable* infant, an infant *capable of survival outside the mother's womb*. Therefore, unless we want to be arbitrary – and it is surely arbitrary to suggest that whether one has inherent dignity depends on *where* one is located: inside the mother's womb? outside it? – we who affirm that every born human

[22] See Perry, Toward a Theory of Human Rights, n. 20, at 7–29.

being has inherent dignity should also affirm that *at least* every unborn human being beyond the stage of fetal development known as "viability" has inherent dignity. In January 1998, *The New York Times* reported that because of advances "in neonatology, most experts place the point of fetal viability at twenty-three or twenty-four weeks."[23] The serious question, then, for those of us who affirm that every born human being has inherent dignity, is not whether we should also affirm that every unborn human being beyond viability has inherent dignity. We should: There is no good reason – no nonarbitrary reason – for us not to do so. The serious question is whether we should affirm that every unborn human being has inherent dignity from an even earlier point in pregnancy than viability – and if so, from what point?

Many opponents of abortion claim that the basic moral status that all born human beings have, they have had from the moment of fertilization, or at least from the moment of implantation. (The latter event – implantation – is often, but mistakenly, referred to as "conception.")[24] According to the

[23] Sheryl Gay Stolberg, "Shifting Certainties in the Abortion War," New York Times, January 11, 1998, at 3.

[24] See Mary B. Mahowald, "Conception vs. Fertilization," Commonweal, September 9, 2005, at 40:

> Although these terms ["conception" and "fertilization"] are often used interchangeably, even in papal documents, "conception" refers to the beginning of a pregnancy within a woman's body, when the embryo is implanted within her uterus several days after

morality of human rights, the basic moral status that all born human beings have is inherent dignity. Should we who affirm that all born human beings have inherent dignity also affirm that all born human beings have had this moral status from the moment of fertilization?

Assume that you believe that the ground of one's inherent dignity is that one is a beloved child of God, or is created in the image of God, or is "ensouled" by God. (Each of these propositions – that one is a beloved child of God, that one is created in the image of God, and that one is ensouled by God – is an effort to mediate in words substantially the same transcendent reality, a reality that cannot be captured or contained or domesticated by any particular formula or vocabulary.) Assume, too, that you also believe that one is ensouled by God from the moment of fertilization. Then you should affirm that every unborn human being has inherent dignity from the moment of fertilization.

an egg is fertilized. In contrast, "fertilization" refers to the process by which any embryo is formed either in vivo or in vitro through union of egg and sperm. (Cloned embryos are not formed through union of egg and sperm.) Infertility practitioners and some people who are publicly opposed to abortion (for example, [Utah Senator] Orrin Hatch) support stem-cell retrieval from in vitro embryos on grounds of this distinction, arguing that new life begins at conception or the onset of pregnancy. The Catholic position should be clearly stated as one that opposes termination of the life of any fertilized egg or embryo (even if the latter has been cloned) regardless of whether conception has yet occurred.

But many who believe that the ground of one's inherent dignity is that one is ensouled by God do not have a confident view about precisely when, during pregnancy, ensoulment occurs. One can be a person of deep religious faith without believing that humans can by dint of "reason" penetrate such a mystery. "Even St. Thomas Aquinas, who thought that a soul was infused into the body, could only guess at when that infusion took place (and he did not guess 'at fertilization')."[25]

[25] Garry Wills, "The Bishops vs. the Bible," New York Times, June 27, 2004. For the views of some Roman Catholics on the issue, see Joseph F. Donceel, SJ, "Immediate Animation and Delayed Homonization," 31 Theological Studies 76 (1970); Joseph F. Donceel, SJ, "A Liberal Catholic's View," in Robert Hall, ed., Abortion in a Changing World 39 (1970); Thomas A. Shannon, "Human Embryonic Stem Cell Therapy," 62 Theological Studies 811, 814–21 (2001); Jean Porter, "Is the Embryo a Person? Arguing with the Catholic Traditions," Commonweal, February 8, 2002, at 8; John Haldane & Patrick Lee, "Aquinas on Ensoulment, Abortion and the Value of Life," 78 Philosophy 255 (2003); Robert Pasnau, "Souls and the Beginning of Life (A Reply to Haldane & Lee)," 78 Philosophy 521 (2003); John Haldane & Patrick Lee, "Rational Souls and the Beginning of Life," 78 Philosophy 532 (2003). Cf. Anthony Kenny, "The Soul Issue," Times Lit. Supp., March 7, 2003, at 12.

Consider these passages from an essay that Peter Steinfels, then editor of the Catholic weekly *Commonweal*, published in *Commonweal* in 1981:

> [T]he right-to-life movement is naively overconfident in its belief that the existence of a unique "genetic package" from conception onwards settles the abortion issue. Yes, it does prove that what is involved is a human individual and not "part of the mother's body." It does not prove that, say, a twenty-eight-day-old embryo, approximately the size of this parenthesis (–), is *then and there* a creature with the same claims to preservation and protection as a newborn or an adult.... Although it is not *logically* impossible, for example, to consider the great number of fertilized eggs that fail to

Some religious believers may be tempted to invoke "revelation" at this point, but revelation does not disclose when ensoulment occurs. ("[Saint] Augustine was [not] certain when the soul was infused.... On the whole subject of the origins of life, [Augustine] said: 'When a thing obscure in itself defeats our capacity, and nothing in Scripture comes to our aid, it is not safe for humans to presume that they can pronounce on it.'")[26] So even if you are a theist, you might not have a confident view about when unborn human beings are ensouled by God (or become beloved children of

> implant themselves in the uterus as lost "human beings", a great many people find this idea totally incredible. Similarly, very early miscarriage usually does not trigger the sense of loss and grief that miscarriage does. Can we take these instinctive responses as morally helpful? ... It is simply *not* the case that a refusal to recognize Albert Einstein or Anne Frank as human beings deserving of full legal rights is equivalent to the refusal to see the same status in a disc the size of a period or an embryo one-sixth of an inch long and with barely rudimentary features.

Peter Steinfels, "The Search for an Alternative," Commonweal, November 20, 1981, reprinted in Patrick Jordan & Paul Baumann, eds., Commonweal Confronts the Century: Liberal Convictions, Catholic Tradition 204, 209–11 (1999). Cf. Porter, supra this note, at 8:

> What can we [Catholics] say to convince men and women of good will who do not share our theological convictions or our allegiance to church teaching that early-stage embryos have exactly the same moral status as we and they do? It will not serve us to fall back at this point on blanket denunciations such as "the culture of death." Naturally, these tend to be conversation stoppers. What is worse, they keep us from considering the possibility that others may not be convinced by what we are saying because what we are saying is – not convincing.

26 Garry Wills, Papal Sin 229 (2000).

God, or become in the image of God). Or you might not be a theist.

Even if you fit one of those two profiles – theist without a confident view, non-theist – you might nonetheless conclude not only that there is no good (non-arbitrary) reason for singling out any point between fertilization and viability as the moment when unborn human life acquires inherent dignity, but also that there is no good reason for selecting viability over fertilization as that moment. In that case, you should accept, by default, that every unborn human being has inherent dignity from the moment of fertilization.

But is it true that there is no good reason for singling out any point between fertilization and viability, or viability over fertilization, as the moment when unborn human life acquires the same, or substantially the same, moral status as newborn human life? In his important book, *A Defense of Abortion*, philosopher David Boonin argues – persuasively, in my judgment – that several of the points after fertilization but before birth that some have identified as the moment when unborn human life acquires moral status – implantation (generally six to eight days after fertilization); actual fetal movement (between five and six weeks after fertilization); perceived fetal movement, or quickening (approximately sixteen to seventeen weeks after fertilization); and viability – are not plausible candidates for the moment when unborn human life acquires moral status.[27] In Boonin's judgment, however, which he defends in an interesting, complex argument, there is a moment after fertilization but before birth when unborn human life acquires moral status: the moment when the fetus begins to display "organized cortical brain activity."[28]

Boonin reports that "there is no evidence to suggest that [organized cortical brain activity] occurs prior to approximately the 25th week of gestation, and ample evidence to suggest that it does begin to occur sometime between the 25th and 32nd week."[29] This means that the point when organized cortical brain activity begins to occur is not a point *between* fertilization and viability; it is a point *after* viability: Again, fetal viability occurs at twenty-three or twenty-four weeks. Boonin's argument supports the proposition that if we want to be cautious, we should assume that every fetus that has reached the twenty fifth week of pregnancy has moral status. But I have aready explained why we who affirm that every born human being has inherent dignity should affirm that at least every fetus that has reached the twenty third week of pregnancy – viability – has inherent dignity. Therefore, we should not select the emergence of "organized cortical brain activity" (OCBA) over viability as the moment when

[27] See David Boonin, A Defense of Abortion 91–115 & 129–32 (2003).
[28] See id. at 115–29.
[29] Id. at 115.

unborn human life acquires inherent dignity. Imagine two viable fetuses whose OCBA has not yet emerged – they are of the same gestational age; the first has been born, the second has not. It seems quite arbitrary for us who affirm that every born human being has inherent dignity to hold that although the first fetus has inherent dignity, the second lacks it.

In any event, there is a second, independent reason why Boonin's selection of the emergence of OCBA as the point at which unborn human life acquires moral status is problematic. In Boonin's argument, desires play the fundamental role: According to Boonin, one human being is the moral equal of another human being at least partly in virtue of having desires, and to respect another human being as a moral equal is to respect his desires – that is, his "ideal" (as distinct from "actual"), "dispositional" (as distinct from "occurent") desires.[30] But, as Boonin explains, a fetus has no desires – in the relevant sense of "desires" – before the emergence of OCBA. However, according to a different argument that is at least as plausible as Boonin's, to respect another human being as a moral equal is to respect not his *desires*, not even his ideal, dispositional desires, but his (authentic)

[30] For his careful presentation of the argument, one should read Boonin's impressive book.

well-being – or, as it is sometimes put, his *welfare*.[31] And even before the emergence of OCBA, unborn human life has well-being, even if in some cases that well-being happens to be compromised in one or more respects.[32]

I said that we who affirm that every born human being has inherent dignity should affirm that at least every fetus that has reached the twenty-third week of pregnancy – viability – has inherent dignity. Notice the "at least." If we affirm that every

[31] See David DeGrazia, "Identity, Killing, and the Boundaries of Our Existence," 31 Philosophy & Public Affairs 414, 428–30 (2003).

[32] See Jeff McMahan, "Paradoxes of Abortion and Prenatal Injury," 116 Ethics 625, 627 (2006):

> Some philosophers argue that a fetus cannot have an interest in continuing to live because it lacks a desire – and even the capacity to desire – to continue to live. But this view is hard to sustain. If a fetus is killed, it will have had a short life containing little of value. Suppose that if it is not killed, it will have a long life containing a great deal of value. The longer life would be the better life. Since each possible life would be the life of one and the same individual, it is better for that individual to have the better of the two lives. But if it would be better *for the fetus* to have the better of the two lives, it is hard to deny that the fetus has an interest in continuing to live.

Assume that for a human being that, like a post-OCBA fetus, has desires, respecting his ideal, dispositional desires and respecting his well-being amount to the same thing as a practical matter, because his fundamental ideal, dispositional desire is to achieve, to the greatest extent possible, well-being. Nonetheless, for a pre-OCBA fetus, respecting his ideal, dispositional desires and respecting his well-being cannot amount to the same thing: The former is an impossible feat, the latter is not. One cannot respect a pre-OCBA fetus's desires; a pre-OCBA fetus has no desires. But one *can* respect a pre-OCBA fetus's well-being – by not acting to impair or destroy, or by acting to protect or improve, the fetus's well-being.

born human being and every viable unborn human being has inherent dignity, and if we can discern no good reason for singling out any point between fertilization and viability, or viability over fertilization, as the moment when unborn human beings acquire inherent dignity, then we should accept, by default, that every unborn human being has inherent dignity from the moment of fertilization. Boonin is right, in my judgment, that there is no good reason for singling out any point between fertilization and the emergence of "organized cortical brain activity" as the moment when unborn human life acquires moral status.[33] *A fortiori*, there is no good reason for singling out any point between fertilization and viability, or viability over fertilization, as the moment when unborn human life acquires inherent dignity. So we who affirm that every born human being has inherent dignity can also reasonably affirm not only that every viable fetus has inherent dignity but also that every pre-viable fetus has it too.

Sometimes conclusions are counterintuitive; this one, however, is not: Why should we think that when an unborn human being becomes viable – capable of survival outside the mother's womb – is relevant to the question whether he has inherent dignity? Why should we think that a six-month-old

[33] But cf. Mary Warnock, An Intelligent Person's Guide to Ethics 43–49 (1998) (giving reasons for drawing the line at "fourteen days from fertilisation").

fetus, because it is capable of surviving outside its mother's womb, has inherent dignity, but that a five-month-old fetus, because it is not yet capable of surviving outside its mother's womb, does not have inherent dignity? Why should we think that one lacks inherent dignity just because one cannot yet survive outside the womb in which one has been gestating?[34] I cannot discern a satisfactory answer.[35] Readers who think they can should take a look at the note accompanying this sentence.[36]

[34] "We can distinguish between being dependent on a particular person and being dependent on some person or other. The viability criterion maintains that the former property[, not the latter,] is morally relevant..." Boonin, n. 27, at 130. "The proponent of the viability criterion is best understood as claiming that a fetus is viable if the technological means of keeping it alive outside of the womb are in principle available somewhere, even if not to this particular fetus." Id. at 131–32.

[35] See John Langan, "Observations on Abortion and Politics," America, October 25, 2004: "[O]ur increased knowledge of embryology and human genetics...[make] clear the continuity and identity of human life from conception forward..."

[36] Consider what Chris Eberle said in written comments on a draft of this chapter:

> [T]he viability threshold makes the inherent dignity of human beings depend[] on temporal and perhaps spatial facts that are every bit as arbitrary as the spatial facts that scuttled the birth criterion. Why?
>
> There doesn't seem to be any reason to believe that we can't develop technology that enables us to keep unborn human beings alive and developing long enough for them to [survive] outside the mother's womb *at any point from conception to birth*. We might not now be able to do so, but of what moral relevance is that? In fact, to claim that it's relevant is to claim that whether one has inherent dignity depends on when one happens to be lucky enough to be born. If we do not now have the requisite technology, but we develop that technology in ten years, then it will turn

It bears emphasis, then, that some of us who affirm that all unborn human beings, pre-viable as well as viable, have

out that unborn human [beings] will be viable, and thus have inherent dignity, from conception on in ten years, but that those conceived now are just flat out of luck. Their clock doesn't start ticking till they're 24 weeks old. It's not clear that this kind of temporal arbitrariness is any less objectionable than the spatial arbitrariness that scuttled the birth criterion.

Moreover, the viability criterion might be arbitrary in much the same way as the birth criterion. Consider a human being who would be able to live outside the mother's womb if that human being were conceived in the USA, but who happens to live in Darfur, which utterly lacks the technology that keeps American unborns alive. Is that child viable? It's not clear: must life – sustaining technology actually be available or must it be available only in principle?

Suppose you take the former route – well, that seems arbitrary in the extreme. Whether one has inherent dignity seems to depend on chance facts about where one happens to be born.

Suppose that you take the latter route – the in-principle available route. Someone, somewhere has the technology necessary to [enable survival] outside the mother's womb. But this seems crazy: what if there are Aliens on another planet with the right technology, but who are not able to get that technology to us any more effectively than Americans can get their technology to the folks in Darfur? Are all unborn human beings viable from conception on if there are Aliens who live on Alpha Centauri who have the technology to keep babies alive from conception on until they [survive] outside the mother's womb?

Maybe not – the technology has to be located here on earth – or at least in our solar system. Well, this is not going to work: do unborn human beings acquire human dignity if an Alien spaceship happens to pass through our solar system (or atmosphere) with the requisite technology? Even if we don't know they are passing through? So unborn [human beings] lose their inherent dignity when the Aliens leave the solar system?

One could spin such silly stories for a long while longer...

You get the picture: making the inherent dignity of a human being depend on viability, which is in turn cashed out in terms of the existence and distribution of technology, is objectionably arbitrary.

inherent dignity do so simply because we can discern no good reason – no non-arbitrary reason – not to affirm it, given that we *already* affirm that all born human beings have inherent dignity. ("The strongest case for personhood *ab initio* I have heard argues from the fact that there is no stage of nascent development that is so significant that it points to a major qualitative change: not implantation, not quickening, not viability, not birth.")[37] Now, one can certainly inquire, as I have elsewhere, at length, *why* one should affirm – *on what basis* one should affirm – that all born human beings have inherent dignity.[38] But the fact of the matter is that many of us *do* affirm it; for whatever reason, or for no articulable reason, we *do* affirm the morality of human rights. And the question for us is that *given* that we affirm that all born human beings have inherent dignity, is there any good reason not to affirm that all human beings, unborn as well as born, have it too?

What philosopher Michael Wreen has written about what he calls the Abortion Argument applies, with slight terminological modification, to the argument I am making here – that it is an indirect argument for its conclusion, one that simply piggybacks on the claim that every born human

[37] Richard A. McCormick, SJ, Corrective Vision: Explorations in Moral Theology 183 (1994).

[38] See Michael J. Perry, "Morality and Normativity," 13 Legal Theory 211 (2008); Perry, Toward a Theory of Human Rights, n. #, at 7–29 (2007).

being – for example, a two-year-old – has inherent dignity. The fundamental grounds for possession of this moral status, "inherent dignity," are not mentioned, much less explored, in the argument. What this means is that it's a secondary, indirect argument, one that attempts to carry the day without itself tackling any of the weightier issues, both metaphysical and moral, that surround humanity and moral status.[39] Wreen surmises that "such an argument is the best that can be done as far as the issue of foetal status and the morality of abortion is concerned..."[40]

Let me emphasize that I do not deny that one who affirms the morality of human rights can reasonably conclude that every unborn human being has full moral status (inherent

[39] See Michael J. Wreen, "The Standing Is Slippery," 79 Philosophy 553, 571–72 (2004):

> The Abortion Argument offers an indirect argument for its conclusion, one that simply piggybacks on the claim that a given being, a two-year-old, is a human being/person/etc. The fundamental grounds for, say, possession of a right to life are not mentioned, much less explored, in the argument. What this means is that it's a secondary, indirect argument, one that attempts to carry the day without itself tackling any of the weightier issues, both metaphysical and moral, that surround humanity, personhood, moral status, and the right to life. It could be that such an argument is the best that can be done as far as the issue of foetal status and the morality of abortion is concerned...

[40] Id. at 572. Wreen then adds: "...but even so, we can hope for more, and try to find more. I, at least, would feel more confident if there were other, independent, and more fundamental arguments that also lead to the same conclusion." Id.

dignity) not from the earliest stage of its development, but only from some later stage. Nonetheless, the foregoing discussion demonstrates that one who affirms the morality of human rights can reasonably conclude that every unborn human being has full moral status from the earliest stage of its development – and reasonably conclude also, therefore, that a law that bans pre-viability abortions is a law against intentional homicide in the relevant sense and, as such, serves a genuinely public good.

One can reasonably conclude not only that the good that bans on pre-viability abortion aim to serve – the protection of human life from the earliest stage of its development – is a genuinely public good, but also that such bans actually serve that good.[41] (They serve it to *some* extent even though, because

[41] Susan Appleton has argued that bans on pre-viability abortions do not aim to serve the protection of human life from the earliest stage of development. According to Professor Appleton, such "bans principally aim to control women and regulate gender behavior.... To the extent that fetal protection is invoked, it simply allows the gender regulation to remain unacknowledged." Susan Frelich Appleton, "Gender, Abortion, and Travel after Roe's End," 51 St. Louis. U. L. J. 655, 660, 666 (2007). However, both in public political discourse and in academic moral discourse, the principal argument in support of bans on pre-viability abortions has long been that such bans protect unborn human life. See, for example, U.S. Conference of Catholic Bishops: Pro-Life Activities, http://www.usccb.org/profile/issues/abortion/index.shtml; Boonin, n. 27. Now, this is not to deny that some supporters of bans on pre-viability abortions want "to control women and regulate gender behavior." Similarly, some believe that abortions harm women and support bans on pre-viability abortions as a way of protecting women.

of illegal abortions and the availability of legal abortions in other jurisdictions, they do not serve it to the extent the bans' supporters would like.) The serious question is whether one can reasonably conclude that such bans serve the public good *in a proportionate fashion*: Are the costs the bans impose so great relative to the public benefit the bans achieve that there is no reasonable justification – no reasonable case to be made – for the bans? Or, instead, can one reasonably conclude that the public benefit the bans achieve warrants the costs the bans impose? This is a famously controversial – indeed, famously divisive – question.

> [A] claim that has been quietly spreading for decades [is] that abortion harms women. Asserting that abortions are coerced and subject women to emotional and physical injuries, South Dakota prohibited abortion to protect women, the unborn, and what the state calls "the mother's fundamental natural intrinsic right to a relationship with her child."

Reva B. Siegel, "The New Politics of Abortion: An Equality Analysis of Women-Protecting Abortion Restrictions," 207 U. Illinois L. Rev. 991, 992 (2006). See also Robin Toner, "Abortion Foes See Validation for New Tactic," New York Times, May 22, 2007. Nonetheless, both in the United States and in other liberal democracies, neither the aim of "control[ling] women and regulat[ing] gender behavior" nor the aim or protecting women from the harm of abortion is the but-for aim of proposals to ban pre-viability abortions. The but-for aim is to protect unborn human life. As those of us who have been close observers of, or even involved in, the abortion wars for the last generation can attest, but for (a) the belief that unborn human life is inestimably precious and (b) the aim of protecting such life, there would be, in the United States and in other liberal democracies at this time, scant if any call for criminalizing pre-viability abortions.

II. Is it unreasonable to think that bans on pre-viability abortions serve the public good in a proportionate fashion?

What costs do bans on pre-viability abortions impose? (Remember: The anti-abortion laws whose constitutionality is at issue here exempt the abortions listed earlier in this chapter.) This is what the Supreme Court said in *Roe v. Wade*, on its way to ruling that bans on pre-viability abortions violate the Fourteenth Amendment:

> The detriment that the State would impose upon the pregnant woman by denying this choice altogether is apparent. Specific and direct harm medically diagnosable even in early pregnancy may be involved. Maternity, or additional offspring, may force upon the woman a distressful life and future. Psychological harm may be imminent. Mental and physical health may be taxed by child care. There is also the distress, for all concerned, associated with the unwanted child, and there is the problem of bringing a child into a family already unable, psychologically and otherwise, to care for it. In other cases, as in this one, the additional difficulties and continuing stigma of unwed motherhood may be involved.

Did the Court overstate the costs? Richard Posner has suggested that the Court *understated* the costs:

> No effort is made to dramatize the hardships to a woman forced to carry her fetus to term against her will. The opinion does point out that "maternity, or additional offspring, may force upon the woman a distressful life and future," and it elaborates on the point for a few more sentences. But there is no mention of the woman who is raped, who is poor, or whose fetus is deformed. There is no reference to the death of women from illegal abortions.[42]

Undeniably, bans on pre-viability abortions impose great costs on pregnant women who want to have an abortion. A law that forbids a woman to have a pre-viability abortion is very different, in that regard, from, say, a law that requires a motorcyclist to wear a protective helmet, or a dress code that forbids policemen to wear beards. Preventing a woman from having a pre-viability abortion will profoundly affect the shape of her life for years to come, perhaps for the rest of her life. Although he was a severe critic of the Court's ruling in Roe, John Ely cautioned: "Let us not underestimate what is at stake: Having an unwanted child can go a long way toward ruining a woman's life."[43]

However, that the costs bans on pre-viability abortions impose are undeniably great does not entail that one cannot

[42] Richard A. Posner, Sex and Reason 337 (1992).
[43] John Hart Ely, "The Wages of Crying Wolf: A Comment on *Roe v. Wade*," 82 Yale L. J. 920, 923 (1973).

reasonably conclude that the public benefit such bans achieve warrants the costs. But that the costs the bans impose are great *does* mean that the benefit the benefit the bans achieve must be great, too, lest the costs be so disproportionate to the benefit that one cannot reasonably conclude that the benefit warrants the costs. The Court in *Roe* was therefore right to insist that because the magnitude of the costs is great, the magnitude of the public benefit must be great, too – great enough that one can reasonably conclude that the benefit is proportionate to – commensurate with – the costs. As the Court put it in *Roe*, legislation outlawing abortion "may be justified only by a 'compelling state interest,' . . . [and] must be narrowly drawn to express only the legitimate state interests at stake."[44]

Is it reasonable to think that the public benefit achieved by bans on pre-viability abortions is proportionate to the costs imposed by the bans? The principal reason for thinking that the main benefit achieved by bans on pre-viability abortions – that many human beings are saved from destruction – is not sufficiently great to warrant the costs such bans impose is this belief: Unborn human beings do not have full moral status – they do not have inherent dignity – from the earliest stage

[44] 410 U.S. at 155.

of development; they acquire full moral status only at some point well after fertilization.[45] As I just explained, however, one can reasonably conclude that unborn human beings *do* have full moral status from the earliest stage of development.

This is not to deny that there is in virtually all liberal democratic societies, including the United States, a deep and widespread controversy about the moral status of unborn human beings in the earliest stages of development. Moreover, there is little if any reason to doubt that this controversy is enduring. Referring to "philosophy, neurobiology, psychology, [and] medicine," Garry Wills has observed that "[t]he evidence from natural sources of knowledge has been interpreted in various ways, by people of good intentions and good information. If natural law teaching were clear on the matter, a consensus would have been formed by those with natural reason."[46] Still, because there is room for a reasonable difference

[45] See, for example, Michael Gazzaniga, "Op-Ed: All Clones Are Not the Same," New York Times, February 17, 2006.

[46] Wills, "The Bishops vs. the Bible," n. 25. On the the enduring absence of a consensus to which Wills refers, compare Robert P. George & Patrick Lee, "Acorns and Embryos," The New Atlantis, Fall 2004/ Winter 2004, www.thenewatlantis.com/archive/7/georgeleeprint.htm, with Michael S. Gazzaniga, "The Thoughtful Distinction Between Embryo and Human," The Chronicle Review, April 8, 2005. See also Anthony Kenny, "Life Stories: When an Individual Life Begins – and the Ethics of Ending It," Times Lit. Supp., March 25, 2005, at 3. Jesuit moral theologian Richard McCormick foresaw that because of this dissensus about the moral status of the fetus – in particular, about the fetus's moral status during early pregnancy – "public policy [would] remain sharply contentious and the task

in judgments about the moral status of unborn human beings in the earliest stages of development, there is also room for a reasonable difference in judgments about whether the benefit that bans on pre-viability abortions achieve warrants the costs the bans impose – a reasonable difference in judgments, that is, about whether bans on pre-viabilty abortions serve the public good in a proportionate fashion and thereby comport with the Fourteenth Amendment.

How, then, should the Supreme Court respond to the claim that the costs that bans on pre-viability abortions impose – again, *bans that exempt the abortions listed earlier in this chapter* – greatly outweigh the public benefit the bans achieve and therefore violate the Fourteenth Amendment? The Court should remind the claimant that the question *for the Court* is not whether the costs such bans impose outweigh the benefit

of legislators correspondingly complex." Richard A, McCormick, SJ, "The Gospel of Life," America, April 29, 1995, at 12, 13. See also John Langan, SJ, "Observations on Abortion and Politics," America, October 25, 2004: "[T]he fact of continuing and intense public disagreement [underlines] how far we are from having a broad public consensus against the practice [of abortion] and of how difficult it would be to . . . enact a legal prohibition against it." Cf. Clifford Longley, "The Church Hasn't Yet Made a Mature Appraisal of What Democracy Demands," The Tablet [London], May 7, 2005, at 11: "The criminal justice system . . . only works when there is at least a minimal degree of assent by the public to the moral framework in which it operates. . . . [W]hat you have to persuade the majority of is not just that your moral principle is correct but that it is right to insist that the minority which does not agree with it must nevertheless comply with it too."

the bans achieve, but only whether one can reasonably conclude that the costs do not outweigh the benefit. Were the Court to ask whether *in its own judgment* the costs outweigh the benefit, it would be acting like a super-legislature, deliberating *de novo* about an issue that the legislature had already (if implicitly) resolved. If, in the Court's view, the legislature's judgment that the costs do not outweigh the benefit is reasonable, there is no good reason for the Court to substitute its judgment for the legislature's.[47]

Can a legislature reasonably conclude that the costs bans on pre-viability abortions impose do not outweigh the benefit the bans achieve? Yes, because, again, one can reasonably conclude – even if one can also reasonably deny – that unborn human beings have full moral status from the earliest stage of development.[48]

[47] Cf. Jon Stewart, America (the Book): A Guide to Democracy Inaction 90 (2004) (describing *Roe v. Wade*, 410 U.S. 113 (1973): "The Court rules that the right to privacy protects a woman's decision to have an abortion and the fetus is not a person with constitutional rights, thus ending all debate on this once-controversial issue."

[48] In *Roe*, the Court rejected Texas's contention that "life begins at conception and is present throughout pregnancy, and that, therefore, the State has a compelling interest in protecting that life from and after conception." The Court said that "[w]e need not resolve the difficult question of when life begins.... [T]he judiciary, at this point in the development of man's knowledge, is not in a position to speculate as to the answer." 410 U.S. at 159. The right question, however, was not what answer the judiciary, or anyone else, should give, but only whether Texas was constitutionally free to give the answer it did. That others would give a different answer – or no answer – is beside the point. As John Ely wrote, "[t]he problem with *Roe* is not so much that

Even if one can reasonably conclude, as many do – including, year after year, many of my students – that legal bans on pre-viability abortions do not serve the public good *in a proportionate fashion*, it does not follow that such bans violate the Fourteenth Amendment, because one can also reasonably

[the Court] bungles the question it sets itself, but rather that it sets itself a question the Constitution has not made the Court's business." Ely, n. 43, at 943. The Court went on to say that "we do not agree that, by adopting one theory of life, Texas may override the rights of the pregnant woman that are at stake." 410 U.S. at 162. But as Richard Epstein appropriately responded: "It makes no sense to hold in conclusionary terms that 'by adopting one theory of life, Texas may [not] override the rights of the pregnant woman that are at stake.' That formulation of the issue begs the important question because it assumes that we know that the woman's rights must prevail even before the required balance takes place. We could as well claim that the Court, by adopting another theory of life, has decided to override the rights of the unborn child." Richard Epstein, "Substantive Due Process by Any Other Name: The Abortion Cases," 1973 Supreme Court Rev. 159, 182.

The crucial question was this: Why wasn't Texas free – free as a *constitutional* matter, free *under the Fourteenth Amendment* – to proceed on the basis of the assumption that a pre-viable unborn child has the same moral status as a viable unborn child or a born child? The Court did not address that question – or, if it matters, addressed it only in the most conclusory terms. Again, Ely: "The Court grants that protecting the fetus is an 'important and legitimate' governmental goal, and of course it does not deny that restricting abortion promotes it. What it does, instead, is simply announce that that goal is not important enough to sustain the restriction." Ely, supra n. 43, at 942. See id. at 924–25 (explaining why, if the Court wanted to "second-guess legislative balances . . . when the Consitution has designated neither of the values in conflict as entitled to special protection[,] . . . Roe seems a curious place to have begun"). If the correct answer is that Texas and other states are constitutionally free to proceed on the basis of the assumption that a pre-viable unborn child has the same moral status as a viable unborn child or a born child, then the pregnant woman does not have "at stake" the right against a state that the Court had in mind, because there is no such right: a constitutional right to noninterference by the state with her decision to have an abortion.

conclude, as many do, that such bans *do* serve the public good in a proportionate fashion. Again, to say that legislators or other citizens *can* reasonably affirm a premise is to say that rational, well-informed, and thoughtful legislators/citizens *could* affirm the premise. One can reasonably affirm the premise that bans on pre-viability abortions serve the public good in a proportionate fashion.[49]

[49] It is no secret that the principal critics of the Court's decision in *Roe* have been "pro-life" on the question whether pre-viability abortions should be banned. The most powerful critique of the decision, however, was written by someone who did not fit that profile, someone who announced, in his critique, that "as a legislator" he would "vote for a statute very much like the one the Court ends up drafting." See Ely, n. 43. (The quoted language is at p. 926.) Ely's unequivocal judgment – delivered in April 1973, just three months after the Court decided Roe – was that the Court's ruling in Roe is "a very bad decision[,]... because it is bad constitutional law, or rather because it is *not* constitutional law and gives almost no sense of an obligation to try to be." Id. at 947.

Ely is not the only politically liberal constitutional scholar who charged that the Court's decision in *Roe* was illegitimate. In 1976, Archibald Cox, who served as Solicitor General of the United States under Presidents Kennedy and Johnson, complained that in *Roe*

> the Court failed to establish the legitimacy of the decision by articulating a precept of sufficient abstractness to lift the ruling above the level of a political judgment... Nor can I articulate such a principle – unless it be that a State cannot interfere with individual decisions relating to sex, procreation, and family with only a moral or philosophical State justification: a principle which I cannot accept or believe will be accepted by the American people.

Archibald Cox, The Role of the Supreme Court in American Government 113 (1976).

In 1979, another liberal constitutional scholar, Gerald Gunther, wrote that although "*Brown v. Board of Education* was an entirely legitimate decision[,]... I have not yet found a satisfying rationale to justify *Roe v. Wade*... on the basis of modes of constitutional interpretation I

Something Justice David Souter wrote in 1997 is relevant – indeed, determinative – here (though Justice Souter, following established Court doctrine, referred to "substantive due process review" rather than to "privileges or immunities review"):

> [J]udicial review . . . has no warrant to substitute one reasonable resolution of the contending positions for another, but authority to supplant the balance already struck between the contenders only when it falls outside the realm of the reasonable. . . . [It is] essential to the intellectual discipline of substantive due process review [to understand] the basic need to account for the two sides in the controversy and to respect legislation within the zone of reasonableness. . . . It is no justification for judicial intervention merely to identify a reasonable resolution of contending values that differs from the terms of the legislation under review. It is only when the legislation's justifying principle, critically valued, is so far from being commensurate with the individual interest as to be arbitrarily or pointlessly applied that the statute must give way. Only if this standard points against the statute can the individual claimant be said to have a constitutional right.[50]

consider legitimate." Gerald Gunther, "Some Reflections on the Judicial Role: Distinctions, Roots, and Prospects," 1979 Washington U. L. Q. 817, 819.

50 Washington v. Glucksberg, 521 U.S. 702, 764–65, 768 (1997) (Souter, J., concurring in the judgment). Compare this statement by the Canadian Supreme Court:

I argued in Chapter 3 that one can reasonably conclude that capital punishment is unconstitutional; I also argued, however, that a Supreme Court committed to Thayerian deference should not so rule. I argued in Chapter 4 that one can reasonably conclude that state refusals to extend the benefit of law to same-sex unions are unconstitutional – and, moreover, that even a Supreme Court committed to Thayerian deference may so rule. I have argued in this chapter that one can reaonably conclude that state bans on pre-viability abortions (bans that exempt the abortions listed earlier in this chapter) are not unconstitutional – and, therefore, that a Supreme Court committed to Thayerian deference should not rule against such bans.

To forestall possible misunderstanding, let me emphasize two things. First, nothing I have said in this chapter entails that state bans on pre-viability abortions are, all things considered, good public policy. (That a law is not unconstitutional does not mean that the law is good public policy.) Indeed, for a lawmaker who does not believe that unborn

> Parliament has enacted this legislation after a long consultation process that included a consideration of the constitutional standards outlined by this Court... While it is the role of the Court to specify such standards, there may be a range of permissible regimes that can meet these standards. It goes without saying that this range is not confined to the specific rule adopted by the Court pursuant to its competence in the common law.

Regina v. Mills, 3 S.C.R. 668 at para. 59 (1999).

human beings, prior to viability, have sufficient moral status to warrant a ban on their killing, presumably such bans are bad public policy. Second, as I have explained elsewhere, even a lawmaker who believes that all human life, unborn as well as born, has inherent dignity can reasonably decline to support the criminalization of pre-viability abortions.[51]

[51] See Perry, Toward a Theory of Human Rights, n. 20, at 59–64.

CHAPTER SIX

Thayerian Deference Revisited

> The ultimate arbiter of what is rational and permissible is indeed always the courts, so far as litigated cases bring the question before them. This leaves to our courts a great and stately jurisdiction. It will only imperil the whole of it if it is sought to give them more. *They must not step into the shoes of the law-maker*...
>
> – James Bradley Thayer[1]

Let's now return to the question with which Chapter 2 concluded:

> In exercising its great power to protect constitutionally entrenched human rights, should the Supreme Court

[1] James B. Thayer, "The Origin and Scope of the American Doctrine of Constitutional Law," 7 Harvard L. Rev. 129, 152 (1893) (emphasis added).

of the United States proceed deferentially; in a case in which it is claimed that a law violates a constitutionally entrenched human right, should the Supreme Court, as Thayer counselled, inquire merely whether the counter-claim that the law does not violate the right is reasonable – and if the Court answers yes, uphold the law? Or, instead, should the Court determine for itself whether the law violates the right – and if it answers yes, strike down the law?

Richard Posner recently observed, approvingly, that "American judges distinguish between how they might vote on a statute if they were legislators and whether the statute is unconstitutional; they might think it a bad statute yet uphold its constitutionality."[2] Thayer urged American judges to make a further distinction: between whether the statute is unconstitutional and whether the claim that the statute is not unconstitutional is reasonable. The latter question, Thayer insisted, is the one judges should address. For Posner, judges usurp the legislators' authority if instead of asking whether a statute is unconstitutional they ask whether it is bad; for Thayer, judges usurp the legislators' authority – they "step into the shoes of the law-maker" – if instead of asking whether the claim

[2] Richard A. Posner, "Enlightened Despot," New Republic, April 23, 2007, at 53, 55. Posner has himself been an "American judge" for over a quarter of a century. Cf."Commemorating Twenty-Five Years of Judge Richard A. Posner," 74 U. Chicago L. Rev. 1641–1931 (2007).

that the statute is not unconstitutional is reasonable they ask whether in their own judgment the statute is unconstitutional. Judge Posner's position, understood as a statement not only about what American judges do *but should do*, represents the conventional wisdom. Professor Thayer's position, by contrast, goes well beyond the conventional wisdom.

Nonetheless, Thayer's position appears quite moderate next to the position Jeremy Waldron espouses. Waldron does not oppose, indeed he supports, constitutionalizing certain important rights;[3] however, Waldron argues that the citizens of "a free and democratic society" should not give to their courts the power to protect (enforce) the constitutionalized rights; more precisely, he argues that they should not give to their courts the power exercised by the Supreme Court of the United States – namely, the power of judicial ultimacy.[4] According to Waldron, the citizens of "a free and democratic

[3] See Jeremy Waldron, "The Core of the Case Against Judicial Review," 115 Yale L. J. 1346, 1366 (2006).

[4] See id. at 1354:

> There are a variety of practices all over the world that could be grouped under the general heading of judicial review of legislation. They may be distinguished along several dimensions. The most important difference is between what I shall call strong judicial review and weak judicial review. My target is strong judicial review.

"Strong judicial review" is Waldron's name for (what in Chapter 2 I called) the power of judicial ultimacy; "weak judicial review," his name for the power of judicial penultimacy.

society should not" as a general matter empower their courts to protect constitutionally entrenched rights because, he says, disagreements about whether a law violates the constitutionally entrenched right it is claimed to violate are reasonable disagreements[5] and there is no good reason to empower the courts to override a reasonable claim to the effect that the law at issue – the challenged law – does not violate the right it is claimed to violate.[6]

[5] See, for example, Waldron, "The Core of the Case Against Judicial Review," n. 3, at 1360, 1368–69, 1406.

[6] Waldron writes that his "argument against [strong] judicial review is not unconditional but depends on certain institutional and political features of modern liberal democracies." Id. at 1353. He allows that strong judicial review may be "necessary as a protective measure against legislative pathologies relating to sex, race, or religion in particular countries." Id. at 1352. "But even if that is so," Waldron continues, "it is worth figuring out whether that sort of defense goes to the heart of the matter, or whether it should be regarded instead as an exceptional reason to refrain from following the tendency of what, in most circumstances, would be a compelling normative argument against [strong judicial review]. . . . What is needed is some general understanding, uncontaminated by the cultural, historical, and political preoccupations of each society." Id. See also id. at 1406.

At one point in his essay Waldron writes: "There may be some countries – perhaps the United States – in which peculiar legislative pathologies have developed. If that is so, then Americans should confine their non-core argument for judicial review to their own exceptional circumstances." Id. at 1386. But how "exceptional" are the United States's circumstances? Are most liberal democracies free of the pathologies to which Waldron refers? Speaking from a British perspective, Lord Scarman, in 1984, wrote: "[I]f you are going to protect people who will never have political power, at any rate in the foreseeable future (not only individuals but minority groups with their own treasured and properly treasured social customs, religion and ways of life), if they are going to be protected it won't be done in Parliament – they will never muster a majority. It's got to be done by the Courts and the Courts can do it only if they've got the proper guidelines." Lord

The fundamental problem with Waldron's position is that in the past, including the recent past, *some* claims to the effect that "the challenged law does not violate the constitutionally entrenched right it is claimed to violate" were not reasonable, and there is no reason to doubt that in the future *some* such claims will not be reasonable. For example, the claim that anti-miscegenation legislation does not violate the Fourteenth Amendment's mandate of equal citizenship is not reasonable; nor is it reasonable to claim that

Scarman, "Britain and the Protection of Human Rights," 15 Cambrian L. Rev. 5, 0 (1984). More recently, and speaking from a broader perspective, Mac Darrow and Philip Alston wrote that "there are ample grounds, based on experience in countries with constitutional human rights protections, to suggest that entrenchment of bills of rights can contribute significantly to the empowerment of disadvantaged groups, providing a judicial forum in which they can be heard and seek redress, in circumstances where the political process could not have been successfully mobilized to assist them." Mac Darrow & Philip Alston, "Bills of Rights in Comparative Perspective," in Philip Alston, ed., Promoting Human Rights Through Bills of Rights: Comparative Perspectives 465, 493 (1999). Such statements are quite common. For example, in a case in which the eleven justices of the Constitutional Court of the Republic of South Africa ruled unanimously that imposition of the death penalty was unconstitutional under the transitional 1993 constitution, the President of the Court wrote:

> The very reason for establishing the new legal order, and for vesting the power of judicial review of all legislation in the courts, was to protect the rights of minorities and others who cannot protect their rights adequately through the democratic process. Those who are entitled to claim this protection include the social outcasts and marginalized people of our society. It is only if there is a willingness to protect the worst and the weakest amongst us, that all of us can be secure that our own rights will be protected.

Quoted in Henry J. Steiner & Philip Alston, International Human Rights in Context 48 (2d ed. 2000).

executing the mentally retarded does not violate the Eighth Amendment's ban on cruel and unusual punishments. Therefore, the following position, which I adumbrated in Chapter 2, is more realistic than Waldron's: Citizens *should* empower their courts to protect constitutionally entrenched rights, and *if* the power they give their courts is the power of judicial ultimacy rather than the power of judicial penultimacy, *then* the courts should exercise their power deferentially, striking down a law only when the claim that the law does not violate the right it is claimed to violate is, in the court's judgment, unreasonable.[7]

In any event, given that for better or worse the Supreme Court has – and exercises – the power of judicial ultimacy, Waldron should want, as second best, the Court to exercise that power deferentially; he should want the Court, in protecting constitutionally entrenched human rights, to take the path of Thayerian deference – and thereby avoid "step[ping] into the shoes of the law-maker."[8]

[7] I have explained elsewhere why the Thayerian argument for judicial deference has little if any power in the context of a system of judicial penultimacy, such as Canada's. See Michael J. Perry, Toward a Theory of Human Rights: Religion, Law, Courts 105–06 (2007).

[8] Similarly, those who advocate on behalf of "popular constitutionalism" – such as Mark Tushnet and Larry Kramer – should want, as second best, the Court to take the path of Thayerian deference. See Mark Tushnet, Taking the Constitution Away from the Courts (1999); Larry D. Kramer, The People Themselves: Popular Constitutionalism and Judicial Review (2004).

One of my two principal aims in the preceding three chapters was to clarify, by modeling, the judicial analysis that Thayerian deference, properly understood, would countenance in particular cases. Chapters 3 through 5 illustrate that Thayerian deference would not emasculate judicial review; judicial review mediated by Thayerian deference would not be so weak as to be, in practice, non-existent. As I explained, even a Supreme Court committed to Thayerian deference should oppose laws and policies such as those struck down in *Brown v. Board of Education* (*de jure* racial segregation)[9] and *Loving v. Virginia*[10] (anti-miscegenation law) – laws and policies that are aspects or remnants of a system of racial apartheid; even a Thayerian Court should oppose execution of the mentally retarded; and even a Thayerian Court has strong grounds to require states to extend the benefit of law to same-sex unions. Clearly, Thayerian deference is no rubber stamp.

Chapters 3 through 5 also illustrate that Thayerian deference is not an algorithm but only a judicial attitude or orientation. Reasonableness *vel non* is a matter of degree, and, again, we should not expect that every judge exercising Thayerian deference will draw the line between the reasonable and the unreasonable at precisely the same point – or,

[9] 347 U.S. 483 (1954).
[10] 388 U.S. 1 (1967).

therefore, vote the same way in a case – as every other judge exercising Thayerian deference. Thayerian deference does not exclude – nothing can exclude – the play of judicial subjectivity from constitutional adjudication. But compared with a non-deferential attitude/orientation, Thayerian deference leaves less room for the play of judicial subjectivity. "Even under Thayer's rule of administration, . . . the freedom and the burden of decisionmaking remain. *But that freedom is narrowed, and that was Thayer's aim*. He sought to reduce the scope of judicial freedom without diminishing the judicial duty and burden of judging."[11]

My second overarching aim in Chapters 3 through 5 was to explain what the implications of Thayerian deference would be for three large constitutional controversies – capital punishment, same-sex unions, and abortion – so that we could then consider whether those implications cast doubt on the proposition that the Supreme Court, in the exercise of its great power to protect constitutionally entrenched human rights, should practice Thayerian deference. It seems to me that the implications not only don't cast doubt on the proposition but strongly support it. No domestic political issues are more morally controversial in the United States today than abortion, same-sex unions, and capital punishment;

[11] Sanford Gabin, Judicial Review and the Reasonable Doubt Test 45–46 (1980) (emphasis added).

indeed, abortion and same-sex unions are at the epicenter of America's culture wars. I have explained why even a Thayerian court should rule that some laws and policies are unconstitutional: executing the mentally retarded, for example. But there is no discernible warrant for the Court's declaring that capital punishment *tout court* is unconstitutional if the legislature's judgment that capital punishment is not unconstitutional is, in the Court's view, reasonable – just as there is no discernible warrant for the Court's declaring that a ban on pre-viability abortions (a ban containing the exceptions I specified in Chapter 5) is unconstitutional if the legislature's judgment that the ban is not unconstitutional is reasonable.

In the United States, Thayer insisted, the citizens are – at least, they are supposed to be – the ultimate political sovereign. Why, then, he asked, shouldn't the citizens, rather than the Supreme Court, have final responsibility for answering, through their elected representatives, contested constitutional questions – so long as their answers are reasonable? Thayer argued that to the extent the citizens are denied that responsibility, they have "cease[d] to function as the popular sovereign."[12] Moreover, "the exercise of judicial review, even

[12] Thayer, "The Origin and Scope of the American Doctrine of Constitutional Law," n. 1, at 87. Something Jeremy Waldron has written is relevant here:

> [T]hink what we might say to some public-spirited citizen who wishes to launch a campaign or lobby her [representative] on

when unavoidable, is always attended with a serious evil – namely, that the correction of legislative mistakes comes from the outside, and the people thus lose the political experience, and the moral education and stimulus that comes from fighting the question out in the ordinary way, and correcting their own errors. The tendency of a common and easy resort to this great function, now lamentably too common, is to dwarf the political capacity of the people, and to deaden its sense of moral responsibility."[13] Thayer concluded that "by adhering rigidly to its own duty, the court will help, as nothing else

> some issue of rights about which she feels strongly and on which she has done her best to arrive at a considered and impartial view. She is not asking to be a dictator; she perfectly accepts that her voice should have no more power than that of anyone else who is prepared to participate in politics. But – like her suffragette forbears – she wants a vote; she wants her voice and her activity to count on matters of high political importance.
>
> [I]magine ourselves saying to her: "You may write to the newspaper and get up a petition and organize a pressure group to lobby [the legislature]. But even if you succeed, beyond your wildest dreams, and orchestrate the support of a large number of like-minded men and women, and manage to prevail in the legislature, your measure may be challenged and struck down because your view... does not accord with the judges' view. When their votes differ from yours, theirs are the votes that will prevail." It is my submission that saying this does not comport with the respect and honor normally accorded to ordinary men and women in the context of a theory of rights.

Jeremy Waldron, "A Right-Based Critique of Constitutional Rights," 13 Oxford J. Legal Studies 18, 50–51 (1993).

13 James Bradley Thayer, John Marshall 106–07, 109–10 (1901). See also Thayer, "The Origin and Scope of the American Doctrine of Constitutional Law," n. 1, at 155–56.

can, . . . to bring the people and their representatives to a sense of their own responsibility."[14]

So, should the Supreme Court take the path of Thayerian deference? Thayer's argument for judicial deference, although quite powerful, does not support the proposition that in every case in which it is claimed that a law violates a constitutionally entrenched human right, the Supreme Court should inquire merely whether the counterclaim that the law does not violate the right is reasonable – and if the Court answers yes, uphold the law. In particular, the argument does not support Thayerian deference – it does not support giving the benefit of reasonable doubt about the constitutionality of a law to the legislators – in adjudicating constitutional questions that fit this profile: *questions such that in adjudicating them, the Court's withholding the benefit of reasonable doubt from the legislators is likely, in the long run, to enhance the capacity of the citizenry either to deliberate about contested political (including constitutional) questions or otherwise to participate meaningfully in the political process*. What constitutional questions fit that counter-Thayerian profile?

In the words of the First Amendment, government may not "abridg[e] the freedom of speech, or of the press; or the right of

[14] Id.

the people peaceably to assemble, and to petition the government for a redress of grievances." Consider questions about the constitutionality of laws and policies regulating speech, press, or assembly: Withholding the benefit of reasonable doubt about the constitutionality of such regulations from the legislators is likely, in the long run, to enhance rather than diminish the capacity of the citizenry and their elected representatives to deliberate in an optimally informed way about contested political questions. In that sense, the logic of the democratic argument that supports opting *for* Thayerian deference in adjudicating constitutional questions of *most* kinds supports opting against Thayerian deference in adjudicating constitutional questions of *some* kinds – namely, questions about the constitutionality of one or another regulation of speech, press, or assembly. In adjudicating such questions, the Supreme Court should not inquire whether the claim, the judgment, that the regulation is not unconstitutional is reasonable; rather, the Court should inquire whether in its own judgment the regulation is unconstitutional – and if it answers yes, strike down the regulation. In short, the Supreme Court should accept and exercise primary responsibility – not secondary (Thayerian) responsibility – for protecting and administering the American system of freedom of expression.

If our concern – the concern that animates the argument for Thayerian deference – is that democratic decision making not be stifled and the capacity for responsible democratic decision making not be subverted, it is better, in cases of reasonable doubt, for the Court, and the courts, to err on the side of less regulation of speech (and press and assembly) than to err on the side of more such regulation. And, as it happens, in the most important speech cases since the 1960s – including *New York Times Co. v. Sullivan,*[15] *Brandenburg v. Ohio,*[16] and *Cohen v. California*[17] – the Supreme Court opted against Thayerian deference; even when it ultimately rejected the constitutional challenge, the Court's opinions in the cases show it asking whether in its own judgment the regulation is unconstitutional. Of course, it is not just in speech cases but in many constitutional cases that the Court's opinions show it asking whether *in its own judgment* the law is unconstitutional. My point here is that in speech cases, at least, it is *proper* that the Court ask that question rather than the (Thayerian) question

[15] See 376 U.S. 254 (1964) (public official may not recover "damages for a defamatory falsehood relating to his official conduct unless he proves that the statement was made with 'actual malice' – that is, with knowledge that it was false or with reckless disregard of whether it was false or not.").

[16] See 395 U.S. 444 (1969) (state may not "forbid or proscribe advocacy of the use of force or of law violation except where such advocacy is directed to inciting or producing imminent lawless action and is likely to incite or produce such action.").

[17] See 403 U.S. 15 (1971) ("absent a more particularized and compelling reason for its actions, the State may not . . . make the simple public display here involved of this single four-letter expletive [fuck] a criminal offense.").

whether the judgment that the law is not unconstitutional is reasonable.

(Two important questions arise here, neither of which I am prepared to address in this book: Should the Court err on the side of less regulation of speech – should it opt *against* Thayerian deference – even when the speech is not political in nature? And if not, how broadly should the category of "political" speech be conceived?)[18]

Are there other sorts of constitutional questions that fit the counter-Thayerian profile: questions such that in adjudicating them, the Court's withholding the benefit of reasonable doubt from the legislators is likely, in the long run, to enhance the capacity of the citizenry either to deliberate about contested political (including constitutional) questions or otherwise to participate meaningfully in the political process? Surely there are: for example, questions that implicate the right to vote. But be that as it may, the issue at hand is whether in adjudicating constitutional questions that do not fit the counter-Thayerian profile, the Supreme Court should take the path of Thayerian deference.

I can anticipate the following objection to Thayerian deference: *As between, on the one side, taking the path of*

[18] Compare Stephen Breyer, Active Liberty: Interpreting Our Democratic Constitution 42 (2005) with Richard A. Posner, "Justice Breyer Throws Down the Gauntlet," 115 Yale L. J. 1699, 1704 (2006).

Thayerian deference in adjudicating questions about constitutionally entrenched human rights (that is, questions that do not fit the counter-Thayerian profile) and, on the other, vigorously protecting the equal citizenship of each and every member of the democratic political community, the Supreme Court should choose the latter. The objection is understandable – but misguided. The Supreme Court need not choose between taking the path of Thayerian deference and vigorously protecting the equal citizenship of all citizens. Again, even a Supreme Court committed to Thayerian deference should have ruled as the Court did rule in *Brown v. Board of Education*,[19] *Loving v. Virginia*,[20] and other, kindred cases.[21] (Any theory of judicial review, Thayerian or not, that fails to account for the rightness – the legitimacy – of the Court's historic ruling in *Brown* is deeply problematic: "The acid test of... any theory of constitutional adjudication is its capacity to justify what is now almost universally regarded as the Supreme Court's finest hour: its decision in *Brown v. Board of Education*.")[22]

[19] 347 U.S. 483. Charles Black wrote that the Supreme Court's historic ruling in *Brown* "opened our era of judicial activity." Charles L. Black Jr., Decision According to Law 33 (1981).

[20] 388 U.S. 1.

[21] See Chapter 4 at 76–77 & n. 17 (discussing *Shelley v. Kraemer*, 334 U.S. 1 (1948), and *Bolling v. Sharpe*, 347 U.S. 497 (1954)).

[22] Gregory Bassham, Original Intent and the Constitution: A Philosophical Study 105 (1992). See also Gerard Lynch, Book Review, 63 Cornell L. Rev. 1091, 1099 n. 32 (1983) ("to most lawyers of my generation, *Brown* is a touchstone for constitutional theory fully as powerful as *Lochner* was for a previous generation"); Mark V. Tushnet,

Moreover, *Brown* and *Loving* are not isolated examples; there are many other cases in which even a Thayerian Court would have had sufficient reason to rule gainst a discriminatory law. Consider, for example, *United States v. Virginia*,[23] in which the Supreme Court ruled that the State of Virginia was acting unconstitutionally – it was violating the Fourteenth Amendment – in refusing to provide for its interested, qualified female citizens a military education substantially equal to the military education it provided for its interested, qualified male citizens. (The Virginia Military Institute, a public institution, admitted only men.) The evidence in the case left no room for reasonable doubt that Virginia's discriminatory policy was based on an ideology – a sexist ideology – about women's proper roles.[24] In that sense, Virginia was treating

"Reflections on the Role of Purpose in the Jurisprudence of the Religion Clauses," 27 William & Mary L. Rev. 997, 999 n. 4 (1986) ("For a generation, one criterion for an acceptable constitutional theory has been whether that theory explains why [*Brown*]...was correct.") For other, kindred statements, see Carlos A. Ball, "The Backlash Thesis and Same-Sex Marriage: Learning from *Brown v. Board of Education* and Its Aftermath," 14 William & Mary Bill of Rights J. 1493, 1516 n. 191 (2006). For a contrarian view, see John Harrison, "Reconstructing the Privileges or Immunities Clause," 101 Yale L. J. 1385, 1463 n. 295 (1992): "I do not think that my theory of the 14th Amendment stands or falls with [its ability to accommodate the Court's decision in *Brown*]. Man is not the measure of all things, as Socrates replied to the Sophists, and neither is Brown v. Board of Educ.... An interpretation of the Constitution is not wrong because it would produce a different result in *Brown*."

23 518 U.S. 515 (1996).

24 Cf. Anna Quindlen, "Not Semi-Soldiers," Newsweek, November 12, 2007, at 90.

some of its citizens as second-class – just as Virginia would have been treating some of its citizens as second-class if it had discriminated against them on the basis of a racist ideology about non-whites' proper roles. So even a Thayerian Court would have had ample reason to rule against Virginia. But perhaps the clearest indication that the objection articulated at the beginning of this paragraph poses a false choice is this: As I explained in Chapter 4, even a Thayerian Court would have strong grounds for requiring states to extend the benefit of law to same-sex unions.

It is simply mistaken to think that the Supreme Court must choose between taking the path of Thayerian deference and vigorously protecting the equal citizenship of all citizens. The Court can do both.

Again: In adjudicating questions about constitutionally entrenched human rights – questions that do not fit the counter-Thayerian profile – should the Supreme Court take the path of Thayerian deference?

Almost fifty years ago, in a book, *The Least Dangerous Branch* (1962), that would become a classic of American constitutional law, Alexander Bickel wrote:

> The search must be for a [judicial] function... which differs from the legislative and executive functions;... which can be so exercised as to be acceptable in a society that generally shares Judge [Learned] Hand's satisfaction in

> a "sense of common venture"; which will be effective when needed; and whose discharge by the courts will not lower the quality of the other departments' performance by denuding them of the dignity and burden of their own responsibility.[25]

My overarching concern in this book has been the proper role of the United States Supreme Court in enforcing constitutionally entrenched human rights. In my judgment, judicial review tempered by Thayerian deference meets Bickel's compelling specifications more closely than does any alternative that has been proposed in the half century since *The Least Dangerous Branch* was published.[26]

[25] Alexander M. Bickel, The Least Dangerous Branch: The Supreme Court at the Bar of Politics 24 (1962).

[26] There are indications, here and there, that support for judicial review tempered by Thayerian deference is growing. Consider, for example, these two recent statements:

> [T]he same Condorcetian arguments that common-law constitutionalists deploy against originalism also support judicial deference to the views of current legislatures. . . . [T]he logical consequence of the informational interpretation of Burke is not robust judicial review, in the style of the Warren Court; rather it is deference to legislative judgments. On this account, Burke leads via Condorcet to James Bradly Thayer, who argued for judicial deference to current legislatures in all but the clearest cases of legislative mistake. . . . The first virtue of any theory of constitutional adjudication is a theory of judicial review – of judicial power to override legislative commands. But the very mechanisms that common-law constitutionalists invoke in praise of constitutional precedent cast legislation in a better light still. If many judicial minds are better than one or a few, many legislative minds are plausibly best of all.

Predictably, not everyone will agree. Constitutional theory is an arena of intense, unrelenting disagreement. Still, the power of the case for Thayerian defence is undeniable, and so constitutional scholars should stop writing as if an argument that a law is unconstitutional is also, if implicitly, an argument that the Supreme Court should so rule (or was justified in so ruling). Even if the claim that a law violates a constitutionally entrenched human right is a reasonable claim, it does not follow that the Supreme Court should rule that the law violates the right. The counterclaim that the law does not violate the right may be reasonable too. And if the counterclaim is reasonable, why should we think it legitimate for the Court to rule that the law violates the right?

Adrian Vermeule, "Common Law Constitutionalism and the Limits of Reason," 107 Columbia L. Rev. 1482, 1506, 1532 (2007).

> On *The New Republic's* website, Cass R. Sunstein has lamented "the absence of anything like a heroic vision on the Court's left" to counteract "the existence of such a vision on the Court's right," embodied by Scalia and Thomas. Here I respectfully disagree. There is, in fact, a heroic vision on the Court's left, and it is squarely in the tradition of previous liberal visionaries like Oliver Wendell Holmes and Louis Brandeis. This vision, championed by [*The New Republic*] since its founding in the Progressive era, is rooted in strenuous bipartisan judicial restraint. It is today defended most eloquently and systematically by Breyer and Ginsburg, who have voted to strike down fewer state and federal laws combined than any of their colleagues.... Judges by their willingness to defer to legislatures, liberals are now the party of judicial restraint.

Jeffrey Rosen, "Court Approval: Will John Roberts Ever Get Better?" The New Republic, July 23, 2007.

Postscript: Religion as a Basis of Lawmaking? Herein of the Non-establishment of Religion

The question whether in a liberal democracy religion – religious rationales – may serve as a basis of (coercive) lawmaking must be disaggregated into two distinct questions: First, is religion a *morally* legitimate basis of lawmaking in a liberal democracy? Second, is religion a *constitutionally* legitimate basis of lawmaking in the United States? I have addressed (elsewhere) the first question[1] – as have many others.[2] In

[1] I have changed my mind over the years. See Michael J. Perry, Love and Power: The Role of Religion and Morality in American Politics (1991); Michael J. Perry, Religion in Politics: Constitutional and Moral Perspectives (1997); Michael J. Perry, Under God? Religious Faith and Liberal Democracy (2003).

[2] See, for example, Richard John Neuhaus, The Naked Public Square: Religion and Politics in America (2d ed. 1986); Kent Greenawalt, Religious Convictions and Political Choice (1988); Stephen L. Carter, The Culture of Disbelief (1993); Robert Audi & Nicholas Wolterstorff, Religion in the Public Square: The Place of Religious Convictions in Political Debate (1997); Kent Greenawalt, Private Consciences and Public

my judgment, the answer is yes; and, again in my judgment, the most powerful defense of that answer is philosopher Christopher Eberle's important book *Religious Conviction in Liberal Politics* (2002).[3] This postscript addresses the second question. The second question, which is about constitutional legitimacy, should not be confused with the first question, which is about moral legitimacy.

Reasons (1997); Paul J. Weithman, ed., Religion and Contemporary Liberalism (1997); Robert Audi, Religious Commitment and Secular Reason (2000); Symposium, "Religiously Based Morality: Its Proper Place in American Law and Public Policy?" 36 Wake Forest L. Rev. 217–570 (2001); Christopher J. Eberle, Religious Convictions in Liberal Politics (2002); Terence Cuneo, ed., Religion in the Liberal Polity (2005); Eduardo M. Penalver, "Is Public Reason Counterproductive?," 110 West Virginia L. Rev. 515 (2007).

3 See also Christopher J. Eberle, "Religious Reasons in Public: Let a Thousand Flowers Bloom, but Be Prepared to Prune" (unpublished ms. 2007). Indeed, given a recent paper by Gerald Gaus, in which he agrees with Eberle that citizens and their elected representatives may rely solely on religious reasons in making political choices, I am inclined to think that the debate is largely over. See Gerald F. Gaus, "The Place of Religious Belief in Public Reason Liberalism" (unpublished ms. 2007). (The two papers just cited, by Eberle and Gaus, were presented at the annual meeting of the American Philosophical Association, Eastern Division, December 2006, Washington, DC.) See also Jürgen Habermas, "Religion in the Public Sphere," 14 European Journal of Philosophy 1 (2006); Virgil Nemoianu, "The Church and the Secular Establishment: A Philosophical Dialog between Joseph Ratzinger and Jürgen Habermas," 9 Logos 17, (2006):

> In a clear and unmistakable manner Habermas condemns all those who keep trying to sentence the religious discourse in the public square to silence, to eliminate and liquidate it all together. "It is in the best interest of the constitutional state to act considerately (*schonend*) toward all those cultural sources out of which civil solidarity and norm consciousness are nourished." Communicativeness implies necessarily and by its very definition the effort of mutual understanding.

Like other liberal democracies, the United States is committed to the right to freedom of religious practice. Unlike most other liberal democracies, however, the United States is also committed to the non-establishment of religion.[4] According to the constitutional law of the United States, government – that is, lawmakers and other government officials – may neither prohibit the "free exercise" of religion nor "establish" religion.[5] Does the non-establishment norm (as I like to

[4] Like the United States, France is constitutionally committed to the non-establishment of religion, which in France is called "laïcité." See Cécile Laborde, "Secular Philosophy and Muslim Headscarves in Schools," 13 J. Political Philosophy 305, 308 (2005):

> On 11 December 1905, republicans in power [in France] abolished the *Concordat* which, since 1801, had regulated the relationships between the French state and "recognized religions" and had, in practice, entrenched the political and social power of the dominant Catholic Church. The first two articles of the 1905 Law of Separation between Church and State read:
>
> Article 1. The Republic ensures freedom of conscience. It guarantees the free exercise of religions.
>
> Article 2. It neither recognises nor subsidises any religion.
>
> The principle of separation between church and state has since been recognized as a quasi constitutional principle, and is implicitly referred to in Article 1 of the 1946 Constitution, according to which "France is an indivisible, *laïque*, democratic and social republic."

[5] The First Amendment to the United States Constitution states: "Congress shall make no law respecting an establishment of religion, or prohibiting the free exercise thereof…" I concur in Kent Greenawalt's judgment that "[b]y far the most plausible reading of the original religion clauses – based on their text, the history leading up to their enactment, and legislation enacted by Congress – is that Congress could protect but not impair free exercise in carrying out its delegated powers for the entire country and within exclusively federal domains, that Congress could neither establish a religion within the states nor interfere with state establishments [of religion], and that Congress

call it) ban religion as a basis of lawmaking? More precisely, should the non-establishment norm be understood to ban laws (and policies) for which the only discernible rationale – or, at least, the only discernible rationale other than an *implausible* secular rationale – is religious? (As I explained in Chapter 4, an implausible secular rationale – a secular rationale that rational, well-informed, and thoughtful fellow citizens could not affirm – is constitutionally inadequate.) *R* is

could not establish religion within exclusively federal domains." Kent Greenawalt, "Common Sense about Original and Subsequent Understandings of the Religion Clauses," 8 J. Constitutional Law 479, 511 (2005). See also id. at 491.

The religion clauses have long been held to apply – it is constitutional bedrock that they apply – not just to Congress but to the entire national government, and not just to the national government but to state governments as well. In effect, then, the clauses provide that government may neither establish religion nor prohibit the free exercise thereof. See Michael W. McConnell, "Accommodation of Religion: An Update and Response to the Critics," 60 George Washington L. Rev. 685, 690 (1992): "The government may not 'establish' religion and it may not 'prohibit' religion." McConnell explains, in a footnote attached to the word "establish", that "[t]he text [of the First Amendment] states the 'Congress' may make no law 'respecting an establishment' of religion, which meant that Congress could neither establish a national church nor interfere with the establishment of state churches as they then existed in the various states. After the last disestablishment in 1833 and the incorporation of the First Amendment against the states through the Fourteenth Amendment, this 'federalism' aspect of the Amendment has lost its significance, and the Clause can be read as forbidding the government to establish religion." Id. at 690 n. 19. (As I have explained elsewhere, a constitutional doctrine is constitutional bedrock if the doctrine is well-settled and there is no significant support – in particular, among the political elites – for abandoning the doctrine. See Michael J. Perry, We the People: The Fourteenth Amendment and the Supreme Court 19–23 (1999).)

the only discernible rationale for a law if but for R – if in the absence of R the law would not have been enacted.

As far as I can tell, there is a virtual consensus among us citizens of the United States, *including those of us who are religious believers*, that, all things considered, it is good both for religions and for social harmony that our lawmakers are constitutionally forbidden to establish religion. The serious question among us, therefore, is not whether the constitutional law of the United States should include the non-establishment norm *but what the non-establishment norm should be understood to mean – to forbid – in one or another context.*[6] In this postscript, I ask what the non-establishment norm should be understood to forbid in the context of lawmaking. I conclude that the answer to the question whether the non-establishment norm should be understood to ban laws for which the only discernible rationale is religious, depends: yes, with respect to some religious rationales; no, with respect to others. I also conclude, however, that insofar as the non-establishment norm is concerned, lawmakers are free to support laws – to vote to enact laws – on the basis of any

[6] However, "[o]ne current Justice on the Supreme Court[, Clarence Thomas,]...twice has asserted that the states should be bound by Free Exercise Clause norms, but should not be bound by Establishment Clause norms." Ira C. Lupu & Robert W. Tuttle, "Federalism and Faith," 56 Emory L. J. 19, 49 (2006). See id. at 49–51.

religious rationale whatsoever. Those two conclusions may seem to pull in opposite directions; I explain in this postscript why they do not.

I. The central meaning of the non-establishment norm

The idea of an "established" church is familiar.[7] For Americans, the best known and most relevant example is the Church of England, which from before the time of the American founding to the present has been the established church in

[7] If the idea is insufficiently familiar, see Michael W. McConnell, "Establishment and Disestablishment at the Founding, Part I: The Establishment of Religion," 44 Wm. & Mary L. Rev. 2105 (2003). According to McConnell:

> An establishment is the promotion and inculcation of a common set of beliefs through governmental authority. An establishment may be narrow (focused on a particular set of beliefs) or broad (encompassing a certain range of opinion); it may be more or less coercive; and it may be tolerant or intolerant of other views. During the period between initial settlement and ultimate distestablishment, American religious establishments moved from being narrow, coercive, and intolerant to being broad, relatively noncoercive, and tolerant. Although the laws constituting the establishment were ad hoc and unsystematic, they can be summarized in six categories: (1) control over doctrine, governance, and personnel of the church; (2) compulsory church attendance; (3) financial support; (4) prohibitions on worship in dissenting churches; (5) use of church institutions for public functions; and (6) restriction of political participation to members of the established church.

Id. at 2131. For a sketch of different kinds of religious establishment, from strong to weak, see W. Cole Durham Jr., "Perspectives on Religious Liberty: A Comparative Framework," in Johan D. van der Vyver & John Witte Jr., eds., Religious Human Rights in Global Perspective: Legal Perspectives 1, 19 et seq. (1996).

England[8] (though the Church of England was much more strongly established in the past than it is today).[9] In the United States, however, unlike in England, there may be no

[8] Cf. Akhil Reed Amar, "Foreword: The Document and the Doctrine," 114 Harvard L. Rev. 26, 119 (2000): "Let us recall the world the Founders aimed to repudiate, a world where a powerful church hierarchy was anointed as the official government religion, where clerics ex officio held offices in the government, and where members of other religions were often barred from holding government posts."

[9] How established is the Church of England today? See Cheryl Saunders, "Comment: Religion and the State," 21 Cardozo L. Rev. 1295, 1295 (2000):

> The special status of the Church of England manifests through legal links with the British crown. Under legislation, the reigning queen or king is "supreme governor" of the church and swears a coronation oath to maintain it. As such, the monarch may not be a Catholic, or marry a Catholic, and must declare on accession to the throne that he or she is a Protestant.
>
> This is surprising enough in a western liberal democracy at the end of the twentieth century. But there is more. The monarch also appoints the archbishops and other reigning church dignitaries. Twenty-six of these "Lords Spiritual" sit in the upper house of the legislature, the House of Lords. The British Parliament can legislate for the church and can prescribe modes of worship, doctrine and discipline. And the church has delegated legislative authority in relation to church affairs. Measures initiated by the church may be accepted or rejected, but not amended, by the Parliament and override earlier inconsistent law.

Professor Saunders then states:

> As usual with the British system of government, however, what you see is not exactly what you get. In advising the crown on appointments to church positions, the prime minister draws names from a list provided by church authorities. As a practical matter, Parliament is unlikely to veto legislative measures initiated by the church, or to act unilaterally in relation to other church affairs. Vernon Bogdanor draws attention to a House of Commons debate on the ordination of women priests in 1993, in which several Members expressed the view that the House should not be discussing the view at all.

established church. The non-establishment norm forbids government to treat any church as the official church of the political community. (When I say "any church," I mean to include any range of theologically kindred churches – for example, Christian churches, which, though denominationally diverse, are sometimes referred to in the singular, as "the Christian church".) More precisely, to say that government may not establish religion is to say that government may not privilege any church in relation to any other church on the basis of the view that the favored church is, as a church, as a community of faith, better along one or another dimension of value – truer, for example, or more efficacious spiritually or politically,[10] or more authentically American.[11] In particular,

Id. at 1295–96. Clearly, and happily, that England has an established church does not mean all that it once meant. Nonetheless, that England *still* has an established church remains controversial. See, for example, Kenneth Leech, ed., Setting the Church of England Free: The Case for Disestablishment (2001); Clifford Longley, "Establishment – It's Got to Go," The Tablet [London], May 11, 2002, at 2; Paul Weller, Time for a Change: Reconfiguring Religion, State and Society (2005). Cf. "The Act of Settlement Debate," The Tablet [London], August 11, 2007, at 4; Tim Hames, "It would have been more honest to have called it the Dangerous Catholics Act," The Tablet [London], August 11, 2007, at 5 (the "it" in the title is the 1701 Act of Settlement).

10 More efficacious politically? Imagine: A macchiavellian advisor counsels the powers-that-be – who, let us assume, are atheists – that it would be better for social harmony if there were an established church, and that because the vast majority of the citizens are members of Church A, it makes more sense to establish Church A than Church B or Church C (and so on).

11 As Justice William Brennan once put it: "It may be true that individuals cannot be 'neutral' on the question of religion. But the judgment of the Establishment Clause is that neutrality by the organs of *government*

government may not privilege, in law or policy, membership in any church – in the Fifth Avenue Baptist Church, for example, or in the Roman Catholic Church, or in the Christian church generally;[12] nor may it privilege a worship practice – a prayer, liturgical rite, or religious observance[13] – or a theological doctrine peculiar to any church.

There is no serious controversy among constitutional scholars, jurists, or lawyers in the United States today about the central meaning of the non-establishment norm: The norm centrally means – it centrally forbids – what the preceding paragraph says it forbids.[14] There *are* serious contro-

on questions of religion is both possible and imperative." Marsh v. Chambers, 463 U.S. 783, 821 (1983) (Brennan, J., joined by Marshall, J., dissenting).

12 For an example of a position that privileges the Christian church generally, see "Other Faiths Are Deficient, Pope Says," The Tablet [London], February 5, 2000, at 157: "The revelation of Christ is 'definitive and complete,' Pope John Paul affirmed to the Congregation for the Doctrine of the Faith, on 28 January. He repeated the phrase twice in an address which went on to say that non-Christians live in 'a deficient situation, compared to those who have the fullness of salvific means in the Church.'" Nonetheless, "[Pope John Paul II] recognised, following the Second Vatican Council, that non-Christians can reach eternal life if they seek God with a sincere heart. But in that 'sincere search' they are in fact 'ordered' towards Christ and his Church." Id.

13 Cf. Douglas Laycock, "Freedom of Speech that Is Both Religious and Political," 29 U. California, Davis L. Rev. 793, 812–13 (1996) (arguing that "[a]t the core of the Establishment Clause should be the principle that government cannot engage in a religious observance or compel or persuade citizens to do so").

14 See, for example, Carl H. Esbeck, "The 60th Anniversary of the *Everson* Decision and America's Church-State Proposition," 23 J. L. & Religion (2007–08, forthcoming): "While Americans robustly debate religious beliefs and doctrine, it is the promise that our government will not

versies, however, about what the non-establishment norm forbids – that is, about what the norm should be understood to forbid – beyond what it centrally forbids.[15]

II. Does the non-establishment norm forbid government to affirm religious premises?

Let's turn to one such controversy: *Given its uncontested central meaning, should the non-establishment norm be understood to forbid government to affirm religious (theological) premises?*

There are many different ways in which government in the United States affirms, or has affirmed, one or more religious

throw its weight behind one side or the other of these debates.... The government, rather, is to maintain a form of 'neutrality.'"

15 I have addressed one such controversy elsewhere. See Perry, Under God?, n. 1, at 3–19.

I don't discuss here the non-establishment case law fashioned by the justices of the Supreme Court of the United States. It bears mention, however, that if Justice Clarence Thomas is right, that case law "is in hopeless disarray..." Rosenberger v. Rector and Visitors of University of Virginia, 515 U.S. 819, 861 (1995) (Thomas, J., concurring). Many constitutional scholars have said much the same thing. See, for example, Jesse H. Choper, Securing Religious Liberty: Principles for Judicial Interpretation of the Religion Clauses 174–76 (1995); William Van Alstyne, "Ten Commandments, Nine Justices, and Five Versions of One Amendment – The First. ('*Now* What?')," 14 William & Mary Bill Rts. J. 17 (2005). Akhil Amar has referred to "the many outlandish (and contradictory) things that have been said about [the nonestablishment norm] in the *United States Reports*." Amar, n. 9, at 119.

premises. Here are some prominent examples: In 1954, the Congress of the United States added the words "under God" to the Pledge of Allegiance ("one nation under God").[16] Also in 1954, "Congress requested that all U.S. coins and paper currency bear the slogan, 'In God We Trust.' On July 11, 1955, President Eisenhower made this slogan mandatory on all currency. In 1956, the national motto was changed from 'E Pluribus Unum' to 'In God We Trust.'"[17] The proceedings of many courts in the United States, including the United States Supreme Court, begin with a court official intoning "God save the United States and this Honorable Court."[18] Some states required their public schools to begin the day with Bible reading or prayer.[19] Some state officials, including some state judges, posted the Ten Commandments on

[16] For a history of the Pledge of Allegiance, which makes its first appearance in 1892, see John W. Baer, The Pledge of Allegiance: A Centennial History, 1892–1992 (1992). The story of adding "under God" to the Pledge involves both the Knights of Columbus (a Roman Catholic organization) and post-World War II anti-communism. See id. at 62–63.

[17] Id. at 63.

[18] See Marsh v. Chambers, 463 U.S. 783, 786 (1983): "In the very courtrooms in which the United States District Judge and later three Circuit Judges heard and decided this case, the proceedings opened with an announcement that concluded, 'God save the United States and this Honorable Court.' The same invocation occurs at all sessions of this Court."

[19] See, for example, Engel v. Vitale, 370 U.S. 421 (1962); School District of Abington Township v. Schempp and Murray v. Curlett, 374 U.S. 203 (1963).

government property, such as a public school classroom or hallway, a courtroom wall, or a courthouse lawn.[20] In at least some such instances, government was affirming one or more religious premises. Is the non-establishment norm best understood as forbidding government to affirm any religious premise whatsoever, no matter what the premise?

I am about to sketch two different understandings of what the non-establishment norm forbids. But it bears emphasizing that no sensible understanding of what the norm forbids denies either of these two propositions:

> First, the non-establishment norm forbids government to affirm any religious premise whose affirmation by government would violate the central meaning of the norm. For example, government may not affirm – explicitly or implicitly, directly or indirectly – that Jesus is Lord, or that the Roman Catholic Church is the one true church.
>
> Second, *if* there are one or more religious premises government may affirm – one or more premises, that is, whose affirmation by government would not violate the central meaning of the non-establishment norm – government, in affirming such a premise, may not coerce anyone to

[20] See, for example, Stone v. Graham, 449 U.S. 39 (1980); McCreary County v. American Civil Liberties Union of Kentucky, 125 S.Ct. 2722 (2005); Van Orden v. Perry, 125 S.Ct. 2854 (2004).

affirm the premise or disadvantage anyone who refuses to do so.[21]

Given the central meaning of the non-establishment norm, the first proposition follows as night follows day. We don't need the non-establishment norm to warrant the second proposition; the free exercise norm – the right to the free exercise of religion – is sufficient. As a moment's reflection will confirm, the free exercise norm protects not only one's freedom to practice one's own religion, but also one's freedom *not* to practice, *not* to participate in, someone else's religion or indeed any religion at all. That "negative" freedom – that freedom not to practice a religion one does not accept – includes the freedom not to affirm a religious premise one does not accept.

Now, imagine two different understandings of what, in the context at hand, the non-establishment norm forbids. According to the first, and more restrictive, understanding, government may not affirm any religious premise whatsoever. According to the second, and less restrictive, understanding, government may affirm any religious premise whatsoever whose affirmation by government would not violate

[21] Sharp disagreement about whether government is in fact coercing anyone – or, more generally, about what, at the margin, "coerce" should be understood to mean – is not uncommon. See, for example, Lee v. Weisman, 505 U.S. 577 (1992).

the central meaning of the norm.[22] The more restrictive understanding would make sense only if there were *no*

[22] Bill Marshall has written that "First Amendment law is relatively settled on the theoretical position that explicit state sponsorship of religion is impermissible." It is clear from his article that by "state sponsorship of religion" Marshall means to include the kind of state affirmation of religious premises entailed by state sponsorship of prayer. Marshall cites two cases in support of his statement of what is "relatively settled": Sante Fe Independent School District v. Doe, 530 U.S. 290, 309 (3000); Lee v. Weisman, 505 U.S. 577, 587 (1992). See William P. Marshall, "The Limits of Secularism: Public Religious Expression in Moments of National Crisis and Tragedy," 78 Notre Dame L. Rev. 11, 21 & n. 57 (2002). Now, I don't mean to deny that the Supreme Court's non-establishment rhetoric lends much support, direct and indirect, to the proposition that "state sponsorship of religion is impermissible." (But see Marsh v. Chambers, 463 U.S. 783 (1983).) Nonetheless, the decision in each of the two cases Marshall cites can readily be understood on the basis of the rule – a rule most naturally assimilated to the free exercise norm – that *if* there are one or more religious premises that government may affirm – one or more premises, that is, whose affirmation by government would not violate the central meaning of the non-establishment norm – government, in affirming such a premise, may not coerce anyone to affirm the premise.

Still, I am undoubtedly swimming against the tide of much scholarly opinion in arguing for the less restrictive understanding of the non-establishment norm. For a sampling of that opinion, see Kent Greenawalt, "Five Questions about Religion Judges Are Afraid to Ask," in Nancy L. Rosenblum, ed., Obligations of Citizenship and Demands of Faith 196, 197 (2000) (declaring that "[t]he core idea that government may not make determinations of religious truth is firmly entrenched"); Andrew Koppelman, "Secular Purpose," 88 Virginia L. Rev. 87, 108 (2002) (stating that it is an "axiom" that the "Establishment Clause forbids the state from declaring religious truth"); Douglas Laycock, "Equal Access and Moments of Silence: The Equal Status of Religious Speech by Private Speakers," 81 Northwestern U. L. Rev. 1, 7 (1986) ("In my view, the establishment clause absolutely disables the government from taking a position for or against religion.... The government must have no opinion because it is not the government's role to have an opinion."). But see Steven H. Shiffrin, "The Pluralistic Foundations of the Religion Clauses," 90 Cornell L. Rev. 9, 72 (2004): "[T]he United States Constitution is best interpreted to be consistent with monotheistic ceremonial prayers that do not involve coercion."

religious premise whose affirmation by government would not violate the central meaning of the non-establishment norm. But there are *some* religious premises whose affirmation by government does not violate the central meaning of the norm. A single example will suffice. Since 1954, as mentioned earlier, the Pledge of Allegiance has echoed Abraham Lincoln's Gettysburg Address in declaring that we are "one nation under God." (At Gettysburg, Lincoln resolved that "this nation, under God, shall have a new birth of freedom...") In affirming, with Lincoln, that ours is a nation that stands under the judgment of a righteous God,[23] government is not

[23] The Declaration of Independence, which marks the first formative moment in the emergence of the United States of America, famously relies – explicitly so – on belief in God: "We hold these truths to be self-evident, that all men are *created* equal, that they are endowed *by their Creator* with certain inalienable rights..." (Emphasis added.) If the Declaration marks a formative moment in the birth of the United States, two texts of Abraham Lincoln mark formative moments in the nation's rebirth: the Gettysburg Address and the Second Inaugural Address, which is surely one of the most theologically intense political speeches in American history. "The Almighty," said Lincoln in his Second Inaugural, "has his own purposes. 'Woe unto the world because of offences! for it must needs be that offences come; but woe to that man by whom the offence cometh!'" Lincoln continued:

> If we shall suppose that American Slavery is one of those offenses which, in the providence of God, must needs come, but which, having continued through his appointed time, He now wills to remove, and that He gives to both North and South, this terrible war, as the woe due to those by whom the offence came, shall we discern there any departure from those divine attributes which the believers in a Living God always ascribe to Him? Fondly do we hope – fervently do we pray – that this mighty scourge of war may speedily pass away. Yet, if God wills that it continue, until all the wealth piled by the bond-man's two hundred and fifty years of

treating any church – including the denominationally diverse Christian Church – as the official church of the political community; government is not favoring any church in relation to any other church on the basis of the view that the favored church is, as a church, as a community of faith, better along one or another dimension of value; government is not privileging membership in, a worship practice of, or a theological doctrine peculiar to any church. The less restrictive understanding of what the non-establishment norm forbids in this context makes more sense than the more restrictive understanding, because there are *some* religious premises whose

unrequited toil shall be sunk, and until every drop of blood drawn with the lash, shall be paid by another drawn by the sword, as was said three thousand years ago, so still it must be said "the judgments of the Lord, are true and righteous altogether." With malice toward none; with charity for all; with firmness in the right, as God gives us to see the right, let us strive on to finish the work we are in . . .

Although we citizens of the United States of America don't recite the Declaration, the Gettysburg Address, or Lincoln's Second Inaugural, we *do* recite, frequently, the Pledge of Allegiance. According to the Pledge, the United States of America is a nation "under God": a nation that, as Lincoln insisted in his Second Inaugural, stands under the judgment of a righteous God. Politicians and others are fond of asking God to "bless" America. Lincoln understood that the God who can, in judgment, bless America can also, in judgment, damn her: "He gives to both North and South, this terrible war, as the woe due to those by whom the offence came . . . [A]s was said three thousand years ago, so still it must be said 'the judgments of the Lord, are true and righteous altogether.'"

affirmation by government does not, or would not, violate the central meaning of the non-establishment norm.[24]

Let's look more closely at the less restrictive understanding, according to which, again, having "under God" in the Pledge, or the like, does not violate the non-establishment norm. Would it violate the non-establishment norm, according to the less restrictive understanding, to have "under Christ" in the Pledge ("one nation under Christ") or "In Christ We Trust" (or "Jesus Is Lord") as the national motto, or to begin a session of court with "Christ save the United States and this Honorable Court"? To arrive at the right answer, we must inquire: In adding "under Christ" to the Pledge, is government treating any church as the official church of the political community? Is it favoring any church in relation to any other church on the basis of the view that the favored church is, as a church, as a community of faith, better along

[24] Cf. ACLU of Ohio v. Capitol Square Review & Advisory Board, 243 F.3d 289, 293 (6th Cir. 2001):

> For most of our history as an independent nation, the words of the constitutional prohibition against enactment of a law "respecting an establishment of religion" were commonly assumed to mean what they literally said. The provision was not understood as prohibiting the state from merely giving voice, in general terms, to religious sentiments widely shared by those of its citizens who profess a belief in God. . . . [T]he principal thrust of the prohibition was to prevent any establishment by the national government of an official religion, including an established church such as that which existed in England at the time the American colonies won their independence from the Crown.

one or another dimension of value? It seems undeniable that in adding "under Christ" to the Pledge, government *is* treating the Christian church – the Christian church *as a whole*, though not any particular denomination of it – as the official church of the political community; government *is* favoring the Christian church in relation to other churches and communities of faith on the basis of the view that the Christian church is, as a church, as a community of faith, better along one or another dimension of value. So, according to the less restrictive understanding of what the non-establishment norm forbids, having "under Christ" in the Pledge *would* violate the norm.[25] For government to affirm any religious premise (or premises) that is ecumenical (non-sectarian) as among the great monotheistic faiths – Judaism, Christianity, and Islam – would not be for it to violate the non-establishment norm.[26] By contrast, for

[25] According to the less restrictive understanding of what the non-estabishment norm forbids, affirming one or another version of the Decalogue also violates the norm. See Paul Finkelman, "The Ten Commandments on the Courthouse Lawn and Elsewhere," 73 Fordham L. Rev. 1477, 1480–98 (2005). Cf. Frederick Mark Gedicks & Roger Hendrix, "Uncivil Religion: Judeo-Christianity and the Ten Commandments," 110 West Virginia L. Rev. 273 (2007).

[26] Cf. id. at 274:

> In the recent *Decalogue Cases* [Van Orden v. Perry, 125 S.Ct. 2854 (2005); McCreary County v. ACLU, 125 S.Ct. 2722 (2005)], Justice Scalia conceded that governmment cannot invoke the blessings of "God," or even say his name, "without contradicting the beliefs of some people that there are many gods, or that God pays no attention to human affairs." Nevertheless, Justice Scalia declares that the contradiction is of no constitutional moment, because the historical understanding of the Establishment Clause

government to affirm any religious premise that is sectarian as among the monotheistic faiths would be for it to violate the norm. In affirming any religious premise that is not ecumenical as among Christians, Jews, and Muslims – for example, the premise that Jesus is Lord – government is violating the non-establishment norm, even according to the less restrictive understanding of what the norm forbids.[27]

Why shouldn't we go further and embrace an understanding of the non-establishment norm according to which government may not affirm any religious premise whatsoever? Again, the central meaning of the non-establishment norm does not require such an understanding. Moreover, no historically grounded reading of the norm – no reading grounded in *American* history – supports that understanding, and it is, after all, the *American* Constitution we are expounding. "[The establishment clause] was not . . . understood to be a prohibition against employing generalized religious language

permits government wholly to ignore those who do not subscribe to monotheism. Noting that more than 97% of American believers are either Christians, Jews, or Muslims, Justice Scalia concludes that the government invocation or endorsement of belief in a monotheistic God does not violate the Establishment Clause.

[27] Justice Scalia has opined that "our constitutional tradition . . . ruled out of order government-sponsored endorsement of religion . . . where the endorsement is sectarian, in the sense of specifying details upon which men and women who believe in a benevolent, omnipotent Creator and Ruler of the world are known to differ (for example, the divinity of Christ)." Lee v. Weisman, 505 U.S. 577, 641 (1992) (Scalia, J., dissenting).

in official discourse. The notion that the First Amendment was designed to impose a secular political culture on the nation would have struck most 19th Century judges as absurd."[28] I can discern no good reason either for expecting the Supreme Court to accept and enforce an understanding of the nonestablishment norm that is not historically grounded or for thinking that the Court should accept and enforce such an understanding.[29] It is surely at least a minor virtue of the

[28] ACLU of Ohio v. Capitol Square Review & Advisory Board, 243 F.3d 289, 297 (6th Cir. 2001). Earlier in its opinion, the court quoted the following passage from an article by Steven Smith:

> In approving the establishment clause, the framers had adopted a principle of institutional separation, but they had undertaken neither to impose a secular political culture on the nation nor consented to abandon their own religious values or culture when serving as public officials. Indeed, any such undertaking would have required a seemingly impossible intellectual and psychological surgery. Proclaiming a national day of thanksgiving, or inviting a chaplain to offer a prayer before congressional sessions, were actions of undeniable religious import. But through these actions the government did not intrude into the internal affairs of any church. Nor did these actions confer governmental authority upon churches; Congress did not endow the chaplain with authority to debate, vote, or directly influence governmental decisions. Hence thanksgiving proclamations and legislative prayers were simply not inconsistent with the decision reflected in the establishment clause.

Id. at 297 (quoting Steven D. Smith, "Separation and the 'Secular': Reconstructing the Disestablishment Decision, 67 Texas L. Rev. 955, 973 (1989)).

[29] I began the paragraph accompanying this note by asking why shouldn't we go further and embrace an understanding of the nonestablishment norm according to which government may not affirm any religious premise whatsoever. However, someone may want to ask a question that pushes in the opposite direction: Why shouldn't we embrace an understanding according to which government may

understanding of the non-establishment norm I am defending here – the less restrictive understanding – that it does not entail a conclusion – namely, that having "under God" in the Pledge or "In God We Trust" as the national motto, or beginning a session of court with "God save the United States and this Honorable Court," violates the constitutional imperative that government not establish religion – that most citizens of the United States would greet as ridiculously extreme.[30]

affirm a specifically Christian premise if the premise is non-sectarian as among Christians? The simplest answer: It is constitutional bedrock that government may not affirm such a premise.

An interesting bit of American history here. The National Association to Secure the Religious Amendment to the Constitution was formed in 1864 "to propose the following change to the preamble to the Constitution (in brackets): 'We, the People of the United States, [recognizing the being and attributes of Almighty God, the Divine Authority of the Holy Scriptures, the Law of God as the paramount rule, and Jesus, the Messiah, the Savior and Lord of all,] in order to form a more perfect union, establish justice, ensure domestic tranquility, provide for the common defense, promote the general welfare, and secure the blessings of liberty to ourselves and our posterity, do ordain and establish this Constitution for the United States of America.'" Jay Alan Sekulow, Witnessing Their Faith: Religious Influence on Supreme Court Justices and Their Opinions 125 (2006). The Christian Amendment, as it was called, "was considered twice by Congress: once in 1874 and again in 1894. The House Judiciary Committee rejected the amendment on both occasions." Id. at 126. Other interesting bits of American history are recounted in an op-ed piece by Jon Meacham, the editor of *Newsweek*: "A Nation of Christians Is Not a Christian Nation," New York Times, October 7, 2007.

30 As even those who reject the less restrictive understanding of the non-establishment norm will likely agree, the Supreme Court will not, in any remotely foreseeable future, rule that having "under God" in the Pledge (or "In God We Trust" as the national motto, or the like) is unconstitutional. If the Supreme Court, in a science-fiction scenario, were to so rule, the citizenry of the United States would rush to amend the Constitution to overrule the Court. Cf. Steven G. Gey, "'Under

True, having "under God" in the Pledge, "In God We Trust" as the national motto, and the like, offends some citizens of the United States.[31] But so long as government fully respects one's right to the free exercise of religion, government's

God,' the Pledge of Allegiance, and Other Constitutional Trivia," 81 North Carolina L. Rev. 1865, 1866–69 (2003) (reporting on the virtually unanimous negative response to the federal court's (subsequently amended) decision in *Newdow v. U.S. Congress*, 292 F.3d 597 (9th Cir. 2002)); Evelyn Nieves, "Judges Ban Pledge of Allegiance from Schools, Citing 'Under God,'" New York Times, June 27, 2002; Howard Fineman, "One Nation, Under... Who?" Newsweek, July 8, 2002, at 20. Religious liberty scholar Steven Shiffrin has argued that the United States has evolved from a country that is historically Christian into a country that is "officially monotheistic." See Steven H. Shiffrin, "Liberalism and the Establishment Clause," 78 Chicago-Kent L. Rev. 717, 727 (2003). See also Shiffrin, "The Pluralistic Foundations of the Religion Clauses," n. 22, at 70–73.

> Proponents of a high wall between church and state, who would remove "under God" from the Pledge of Allegiance, are wishing for a country that does not exist and probably never will. Our Constitution must be interpreted in the light of our evolving traditions – like it or not. So we make compromises and today government can say "In God we trust" on its coins but not "In Christ we trust."

Id.

31 Cf. Steven D. Smith, Foreordained Failure: The Quest for a Constitutional Principle of Religious Freedom 164–65 n. 66 (1995):

> [T]he very concept of "alienation," or symbolic exclusion, is difficult to grasp. How, if at all, does "alienation" differ from "anger," "annoyance," "frustration," or "disappointment" that every person who finds himself in a political minority is likely to feel? "Alienation" might refer to nothing more than an awareness by an individual that she belongs to a religious minority, accompanied by a realization that at least on some issues she is unlikely to be able to prevail in the political process.... That awareness may be discomforting. But is it the sort of phenomenon for which constitutional law can provide an efficacious remedy? Constitutional doctrine that stifles the message will not likely alter the reality – or a minority's awareness of that reality.

affirmation of one or more religious premises does not violate anyone's human rights. For example, that the Constitution of the Republic of Ireland makes a number of theological affirmations – while also vigorously protecting every Irish citizen's right to freedom of religious practice – does not violate anyone's human rights.[32] More generally, the international

[32] In its Preamble, the Irish Constitution affirms a non-sectarian Christianity: "In the name of the Most Holy Trinity, from Whom is all authority and to Whom, as our final end, all actions both of men and States must be referred, we, the people of Eire, humbly acknowledging all our obligations to our Divine Lord, Jesus Christ, Who sustained our fathers through centuries of trial, . . . do hereby adopt, enact, and give to ourselves this Constitution." Moreover, Article 6 states, in relevant part: "All powers of government, legislative, executive, and judicial, derive, *under God*, from the people, whose right it is to designate the rulers of the State and, in the final appeal, to decide all questions of national policy, according to the requirements of the common good." (Emphasis added.) And Article 44 of the Constitution states, in relevant part: "The State acknowledges that the homage of public worship is due to Almighty God. It shall hold His Name in reverence, and shall respect and honor religion." On "religion in the Preamble," see Gerard Hogan & G. F. Whyte, J. M. Kelly's The Irish Constitution 6–7 (3d ed., 1994). (Although it affirms Christianity, the Irish Constitution explicitly disallows the "endowing" of any religion. Article 44.2.1 states: "The State guarantees not to endow any religion.")

Given the religious commitments of the vast majority of the people of Ireland, it is not at all surprising that the Irish Constitution affirms Christianity. In so doing, the Irish Constitution violates no human right. Three things are significant here. First, the religious convictions implicit in the Irish Constitution's affirmation of Christianity in no way deny – indeed, they affirm – the idea that *every* human being, *Christian or not*, is inviolable; they affirm, that is, the idea of human rights. Second, the Irish Constitution's affirmation of Christianity is not meant to insult or demean anyone; it is meant only to express the most fundamental convictions of the vast majority of the people of Ireland. Third, and most important, the Irish Constitution protects the right, which is a human right, to freedom of religious practice; moreover, it protects this right not just for Christians, who are the vast

law of human rights features the right to freedom of religious practice but does not include anything like a nonestablishment norm; in particular, the Declaration on the

majority in Ireland, but for all citizens. Article 44 states, in relevant part: "Freedom of conscience and the free profession and practice of religion are . . . guaranteed to every citizen. . . . The State shall not impose any disabilities or make any discrimination on the ground of religious profession, belief or status." Article 44 also states that "[l]egislation providing State aid for schools shall not discriminate between schools under the management of different religious denominations, *nor be such as to effect prejudicially the right of any child to attend a school receiving public money without attending religious instruction at that school*." (Emphasis added.) Therefore, the conclusion that in affirming Christianity the Irish Constitution violates a human right – or that in consequence of the affirmation Ireland falls short of being a full fledged liberal democracy – is, in a word, extreme. For an excellent essay on religious liberty in Ireland, see G. F. Whyte, "The Frontiers of Religious Liberty: A Commonwealth Celebration of the 25th Anniversary of the U.N. Declaration on Religious Tolerance – Ireland," 21 Emory International L. Rev. 43 (2007).

If what Brian Barry says in the following passage is true with respect to England, which has an established church, then it is even more true with respect to the United States, which has no established church but only such comparatively minor things as "under God" in the Pledge and "In God We Trust" as the national motto:

> We must, of course, keep a sense of proportion. The advantages of establishment enjoyed by the Church of England or by the Lutheran Church in Sweden are scarcely on a scale to lead anyone to feel seriously discriminated against. In contrast, denying the vote to Roman Catholics or requiring subscription to the Church of England as a condition of entry to Oxford or Cambridge did constitute a serious source of grievance. Strict adherence to justice as impartiality would, no doubt, be incompatible with the existence of an established church at all. But departures from it are venial so long as nobody is put at a significant disadvantage, either by having barriers put in the way of worshipping according to the tenets of his faith or by having his rights and opportunities in other matters (politics, education, occupation, for example) materially limited on the basis of his religious beliefs.

Brian Barry, Justice as Impartiality 165 n. c (1995).

Elimination of All Forms of Intolerance and of Discrimination Based on Religion or Belief, which is the principal international document concerning religious freedom, includes nothing like a non-establishment requirement.[33]

Is it really the case that the more restrictive understanding of what the non-establishment norm forbids in this context yields the conclusion that having "under God" in the Pledge or "In God We Trust" as the national motto, or beginning a session of court with "God save the United States and this Honorable Court," is unconstitutional? Is there a way for one

[33] From the perspective of the morality of human rights, it is a matter of indifference whether liberal democracies establish religion – so long as they comply fully with the right to freedom of religious practice. See also John Finnis, "Religion and State: Some Main Issues and Sources," http://ssrn.com/abstract=943420 (2006), at 30 (arguing that so long as they comply fully with the right to freedom of religious practice, "in establishing their constitutional arrangements a people might without injustice or political impropriety record their solemn belief about the identity and name of the true religious faith and community"). As a practical matter, then, a liberal democracy may establish religion only in a weak sense of "establish." A liberal democracy may not, for example, discriminate against any of its citizens because they are not members of the established church. As the cardinals and bishops of the Catholic Church stated at Vatican II:

> If, in view of particular circumstances, obtaining among peoples, special civil recognition is given to one religiuous community in the constitutional order of society, it is at the same time imperative that the right of all citizens and religious communities to religious freedom should be recognized and made effective in practice.
>
> Finally, government is to see to it that the equality of citizens before the law, which is itself an element of the common good, is never violated, whether openly or covertly, for religious reasons. Nor is there to be discrimination among citizens.

Dignitatis Humanae, section 6.

who accepts the more restrictive understanding to avoid that conclusion, which, again, most citizens of the United States would greet as ridiculously extreme?

Consider the suggestion that having "under God" in the Pledge or "In God We Trust" as the national motto (or the like) is not unconstitutional because such statements do not really constitute an affirmation by government of a religious premise; instead, such statements are merely patriotic or ceremonial utterances devoid of authentically religious content.[34] In 1983, Supreme Court Justice William Brennan, joined by Justice Thurgood Marshall, wrote:

> I frankly do not know what should be the proper disposition of features of our public life such as "God save the United States and this Honorable Court," "In God We Trust," "One Nation Under God," and the like. I might well adhere to the view... that such mottoes are consistent with the Establishment Clause... because they have lost any true religious significance.[35]

In 2004, Chief Justice William Rehnquist, joined by Justice Sandra Day O'Connor, said something similar: "The phrase 'under God' is in no sense a prayer, nor an endorsement of any religion... Reciting the Pledge, or listening to others recite it, is a patriotic exercise, not a religious one; participants

[34] Cf. Marshall, n. 22, at 23 (discussing "ceremonial deism").
[35] Marsh v. Chambers, 463 U.S. 783, 818 (1983) (dissenting).

promise fidelity to our flag and our Nation, not to any particular God, faith, or church."[36]

Asserting that "one nation under God" or "In God We Trust" are merely patriotic or ceremonial utterances devoid of authentically religious content is obviously a convenient strategy for avoiding the conclusion that under the more restrictive understanding of the non-establishment norm, having "under God" in the Pledge or "In God We Trust" as our national motto is unconstitutional. It is also a palpably disingenuous

[36] Elk Grove Unified School District v. Newdow, 542 U.S. 1, 31 (2004) (concurring in judgment). *Newdow* is the case in which it was claimed that just as having public school children recite a prayer violates the non-establishment norm, so too having them recite the Pledge of Allegiance violates the non-establishment norm, because the Pledge states that the United States is a nation "under God" and recitation of the Pledge is therefore a religious exercise. The U.S. Court of Appeals for the Ninth Circuit agreed, and the case ended up in the U.S. Supreme Court, where

> [s]ix Justices reversed on a procedural ground, arguing that Newdow did not have standing to bring the action. Three justices, however, namely, Chief Justice Rehnquist and Justices O'Connor and Thomas, disagreed with [the Ninth Circuit] on the merits.
>
> Analyzing [the Ninth Circuit's]opinion requires separation of two issues: First, is the Pledge a *religious* exercise, and, second, can a government actor constitutionally require that the Pledge be part of the official public school day? Chief Justice Rehnquist and Justice O'Connor both denied that the Pledge was a religious exercise and, therefore, concluded that it could be a part of the official public school day. Justice Thomas conceded that the Pledge was religious but... argued [that] it was constitutional nonetheless.

Shiffrin, "The Pluralistic Foundations of the Religion Clauses," n. 22, at 65–66. Shiffrin argues "that the Pledge is religious and that it is constitutional for Congress to encourage its use, but that it should not be considered constitutionally permissible to use the Pledge in public school classrooms." Id. at 66.

strategy.[37] There are *some* citizens, no doubt, for whom the statements are merely ceremonial, religiously empty utterances; it is simply mistaken, however, to think that the statements are religiously empty for most, or even for many, citizens of the United States – or that they were religiously empty for the members of Congress who, in 1954, added "under God" to the Pledge.[38] For most Americans, the statements resonate, as indeed they were meant to, with an authentically and rich theological content: that there is a God; that God created us and sustains us; that every human being has a God-given dignity and inviolability; and that, as Lincoln proclaimed in his Second Inaugural, we stand under the judgment of that righteous God.[39]

There is no intellectually honest way for one who accepts the more restrictive understanding of the non-establishment norm to avoid the conclusion that having "under God" in the Pledge or "In God We Trust" as the national motto, or beginning a session of court with "God save the United States

[37] See Richard John Neuhaus, "Nasty and Nice in Politics and Religion in the Public Sqare: A Survey of Religion and Public Life," First Things, March 2004, at 69, 70.

[38] No one with any doubt on this score should fail to read Steven Gey's fine article. See Gey, n. 30, at 1873–80.

[39] See Douglas Laycock, "Theology Scholarships, the Pledge of Allegiance, and Religious Liberty: Avoiding the Extremes, Missing the Liberty," 118 Harvard L. Rev. 155, 224–27 (2004) (arguing that recitation of the Pledge of Allegiance is a profession of faith); id. at 226–27 and n. 458 (noting others who argue that recitation of the Pledge is a profession of faith).

and this Honorable Court", is unconstitutional. For one who is intellectually honest, to accept the more restrictive understanding is to accept that conclusion.[40]

III. Does the non-establishment norm, properly understood, ban religion as a basis of lawmaking?

Now, the question-in-chief: Is religion a legitimate – a *constitutionally* legitimate – basis of lawmaking in the United States? More precisely, should the non-establishment norm be understood to ban laws (and policies) for which the only discernible rationale (at least, other than an implausible secular rationale) is religious?[41] Two clarifications:

> First, the principal laws at issue are those that are coercive, because coercive laws for which the only discernible rationale is religious are a kind of religious imposition on those they coerce.[42] Kent Greenawalt, for example, has

[40] See Shiffrin, "The Pluralistic Foundations of the Religion Clauses," n. 22, at 66–70 (explaining why the positions of Rehnquist and O'Connor in the *Newdow* case [see n. 30] are untenable).

[41] Steve Shiffrin has addressed much the same question and, unless I misunderstand him, has given much the same answer I give here. See Steven Shiffrin, "Religion and Democracy," 74 Notre Dame L. Rev. 1631, 1652–56 (1999).

[42] Cf. Robert Audi, "Liberal Democracy and the Place of Religion in Politics," . . . 32: "[N]on-religious people often tend to be highly and stubbornly passionate about not being coerced to [act in accordance with religious reasons]. . . . [M]any who are not religious are incensed at the thought of manipulation in the name of someone else's nonexistent deity."

written of laws "that enforce a purely religious morality" that "they unacceptably impose religion on others." He gives, as an example, "laws against homosexual relations based on the view that the Bible considers such relations sinful..."[43]

Second, by a "religious" rationale I mean a rationale that depends, at least in part, on a religious premise; a "secular" rationale, by contrast, does not depend on any religious premise. By a "religious" premise I mean, in this book, a premise – a claim – about the existence,[44] nature, activity, or will of God, such as the premise that same-sex unions are contrary to the will of God.[45]

43 Kent Greenawalt, "History as Ideology: Philip Hamburger's *Separation of Church and State*," 93 California L. Rev. 367, 390–91 (2005). See also Kent Greenawalt, "Religiously Based Judgments and Discourse in Political Life," 22 St. John's J. Legal Commentary 445, 487 (2007): "[R]equiring people to comply with the moral code of a religion, absent any belief about ordinary harm to entities deserving protection, is a kind of imposition of that religious view on others." Cf. Stephen Macedo, "Transformative Constitutionalism and the Case of Religion: Defending the Moderate Hegemony of Liberalism," 26 Political Theory 56, 71 (1998) ("The liberal claim is that it is wrong to seek to coerce people on grounds that they cannot share without converting to one's faith."); Robert Audi, "The Place of Religious Argument in a Free and Democratic Society," 30 San Diego L. Rev. 677, 701 (1993) ("If you are fully rational and I cannot convince you of my view by arguments framed in the concepts we share as rational beings, then even if mine is the majority view I should not coerce you.").

44 On non-existence. Atheism is a religious position – a position on a religious question – for purposes of the non-establishment norm. Cf. Derek H. Davis, "Is Atheism a Religion? Recent Judicial Perspectives on the Constitutional Meaning of 'Religion,'" 47 J. Church & State 707 (2005).

45 Cf. Eberle, Religious Conviction in Liberal Politics, n. 2, at 71:

> I shall understand a religious ground... as any ground that has *theistic content*. Paradigmatic religious grounds are, for example,

I argued in the preceding section that according to the most balanced understanding of what it forbids, the non-establishment norm forbids government to affirm some religious premises – but that it also leaves room for government to affirm some religious premises – namely, premises whose affirmation by government does not, or would not, violate the central meaning of the non-establishment norm.[46] It follows from that argument that the non-establishment norm should *not* be understood to ban laws for which the only discernible rationale is a religious rationale that depends on a premise (or premises) government *may* affirm (because its doing so does not, or would not, violate the central meaning of the non-establishment norm), such as the premise that every human being has a God-given dignity and inviolability.[47]

a putative experience of God as affirming racial harmony, the claim that God has revealed in the Bible that homosexual relations are morally forbidden, the testimony of a religious authority that God abhors despoliation of the environment.

46 Although under the non-establishment norm there are some religious premises that government may not affirm – for example, the premise that God created the universe not 6,000 years ago, as some "young-earth creationists" claim, but billions of years ago – government may nonetheless affirm a premise that is consistent with a religious premise it may *not* affirm, so long as government's rationale for affirming the non-religious premise does not rely on a religious premise government that it may *not* affirm. So government may affirm the premise that the universe is billions of years old.

47 Cf. Edwards v. Aguillard, 482 U.S. 578, 615 (1987) (Scalia, J., dissenting): "Our cases in no way imply that the Establishment Clause forbids legislators merely to act upon their religious convictions. We surely would not strike down a law providing money to feed the hungry or shelter the homeless if it could be demonstrated that, but for

It also follows, however, that the non-establishment norm *should be* understood to ban laws for which the only discernible rationale is a religious rationale that depends on – and in that sense affirms – a religious premise government may *not* affirm.

A lawmaker supports a law – she votes to enact a law – "on the basis of" a religious rationale if but for the religious rationale – if in the absence of the religious rationale – she would not vote to enact the law. Put another way, a lawmaker votes to enact a law "on the basis of" a religious rationale if there is no secular rationale that by itself would move her to enact the law.[48] However, the non-establishment ban I am articulating here is indifferent to whether a lawmaker who voted to enact a law *actually* did so, either wholly or partly, on the basis of an "offending" religious rationale – a rationale that depends on a religious premise government

the religious beliefs of the legislators, the funds would not have been approved. . . . [P]olitical activism by the religiously motivated is part of our heritage."

48 Cf. Eberle, Religious Conviction in Liberal Politics, n. 2, at 73:

> Whether [one] supports a given law on the basis of his religious convictions alone depends on the answer to a conterfactual question: would [he] continue to regard moral claim C (on the basis of which he supports a proposed law) as sufficient reason for that law if he didn't believe that theistic claim T constitutes adequate reason for C?

may not affirm. There are several good reasons for that indifference:

- It is unrealistic to expect most lawmakers to have a confident answer to the question whether they would have voted to enact a law but for an offending religious rationale.
- The ban, qua legal, is meant to be judicially enforceable. If most lawmakers themselves don't have a confident answer to the question whether they would have voted to enact a law but for an offending religious rationale, how is a court supposed to know whether they would have done so?
- Moreover, if courts were in the business of speculating about whether the lawmakers would have voted to enact a law but for an offending religious rationale, some lawmakers would respond by engaging in strategic behavior aimed at making it appear that they would have voted to enact the law on the basis of a plausible secular rationale and/or a non-offending religious rationale.
- Finally, consider this scenario: A court speculates that the lawmakers in State A would have voted to enact law L on the basis of a plausible secular rationale, and therefore concludes that L is not unconstitutional, while

> a different court speculates that the lawmakers in State B would not have voted to enact the very same law on the basis of any plausible secular rationale, and therefore concludes that L is unconstitutional. In State A, L is constitutional; in State B, L is unconstitutional. What an unseemly state of affairs that would be!

So the non-establishment norm is better understood as not forbidding a lawmaker to support a law on the basis of an offending religious rationale, but only to ban laws for which the only discernible rationale is an offending religious rationale.

As a practical matter, how significant is a ban on such laws? In the United States today, there are, and in the foreseeable future there will be, almost no actual or proposed laws – at least, almost no proposed laws that have a realistic chance of becoming actual laws – that fit the profile "laws for which the only discernible rationale is an offending religious rationale." For example, and as I explained in Chapter 5, there is a plausible secular rationale – a secular rationale that rational, well-informed, and thoughtful fellow citizens could affirm – for laws banning most abortions. There is one policy, however, with respect to which the ban may have bite: Many states refuse to recognize – they refuse to extend the benefit of law to – same-sex unions. If no plausible secular rationale can account for that policy – if the only rationale that accounts for the policy depends on the premise that same-sex sexual conduct is contrary to the will of God – this becomes the determinative question: May government affirm the premise that same-sex sexual conduct is contrary to the will of God? I addressed that question in Chapter 6, in the course of discussing the controversy over same-sex unions.

As I said at the beginning of this postscript, the principal question at issue here – whether religion (religious rationales) is a *constitutionally* legitimate basis of lawmaking *in the United States* – should not be confused with a different question that has been contested in the United States (and elsewhere) for the last thirty years or so: Is religion a *morally* legitimate basis of lawmaking *in a liberal democracy*; more precisely, is it morally legitimate for lawmakers in a liberal democracy to enact laws on the basis of a religious rationale? Again, the answer to that question, in my judgment, is yes.[49]

Some who give that answer may be inclined to think that the non-establishment ban articulated and defended here – the ban on laws for which the only discernible rationale

[49] See nn. 1–3 and accompanying text.

is an offending religious rationale – is unduly restrictive of religious believers. So let me explain why they should resist that thought:

> First, laws for which the only discernible rationale depends on a religious premise that government *may* affirm, *including the premise that every human being has a God-given dignity and inviolability*, are *not* subject to the ban.
>
> Second, although laws for which the only discernible rationale is an offending religious rationale are subject to the ban, in the United States today there are, and in the foreseeable future there will be, as I just remarked, few if indeed any actual or proposed laws that fit that profile.

The serious question, then, is not whether the non-establishment ban on laws for which the only discernible rationale is an offending religious rationale is unduly restrictive, but whether as a practical matter the ban has much, if any, bite at all.

Moreover, insofar as the non-establishment norm is concerned, a lawmaker is free to support a law on the basis of any religious rationale whatsoever, even an offending religious rationale;[50] she is free to support a law that but for an

[50] This is not to deny that a religious rationale may be inconsistent with the morality of liberal democracy or with one or more constitutional norms other than the non-establishment norm or with both. Consider, for example, the religious claim that in God's created order, some human beings do *not* have inherent dignity.

offending religious rationale – a rationale that depends on a religious premise that under the non-establishment norm government may not affirm – she would not vote to enact.[51] As

[51] Cf. Audi & Wolterstorff, n. 2, at 105 (Wolterstorff writing; emphasis in original):

> It belongs to the *religious convictions* of a good many religious people in our society that *they ought to base* their decisions concerning fundamental issues of justice on their religious convictions. They do not view it as an option whether or not to do so. It is their conviction that they ought to strive for wholeness, integrity, integration, in their lives: that they ought to allow the Word of God, the teachings of the Torah, the command and example of Jesus, or whatever, to shape their existence as a whole, including, then, their social and political existence. Their religion is not, for them, *something other* than their social and political existence; it is also about their social and political existence.

It is sometimes suggested that in liberal democracies – or at least in religiously pluralistic liberal democracies like the United States – it is inappropriate to bring religious arguments about contested political issues into the public square; one should leave one's religious arguments at home and bring only secular arguments into the public square. However, if one concludes – as Chris Eberle and I both do – that religious rationales are a morally legitimate basis of lawmaking in a liberal democracy, then presumably one also concludes that religious rationales may be brought into the public square – that is, that religious arguments are a morally legitimate subject of public political argument. But even if one were to reject the conclusion that religious rationales are a morally legitimate basis of lawmaking in a liberal democracy, one should still conclude that religious rationales are a morally legitimate subject of public political argument: It would make little, if any, sense to discourage lawmakers and other citizens from presenting religious rationales in public political argument, because, like it or not, in some liberal democracies it is inevitable – certainly in the United States it is inevitable – that from time to time some lawmakers and other citizens will support a contested law on the basis of a religious rationale. It is obviously better that the rationale (unless it is politically quite marginal) be critically engaged in public political argument than that it be ignored. See Perry, Under God? n. 1, at 38–44.

it happens, however, the vast majority of religious believers in the United States offer non-religious rationales for their political positions on controversial moral issues. Even "[m]ost religious conservatives do, frequently and loudly, make arguments for their positions *on nontheological grounds*.... [T]he evils of abortion, the value of heterosexual monogamy, the costs of promiscuity and pornography – all these issues are constantly being raised by social conservatives without appeals to the divine inspiration of the Bible."[52] So, again, the serious question is not whether the non-establishment ban on laws for which the only discernible rationale is an offending religious rationale is unduly restrictive, but whether as a practical matter the ban has much, if any, bite at all.[53]

The right to freedom of religious practice is widely regarded as a human right to which every government should

[52] Ross Douthat, "Theocracy, Theocracy, Theocracy," First Things, August/September 2006, at 23, 28 (emphasis added).

[53] John Finnis represents the Roman Catholic Church's view of the relationship among morality, reason, and religion when he writes:

> [I]ndividual voters and legislators can rightly and should take into account the firm moral teachings of a religion if it is the true religion, so far as its teachings are relevant to issues of law and government.... In saying that voters and other bearers of public authority have this liberty, I assume that the true religion itself holds out its moral teaching as a matter of public reason, i.e. as accessible and acceptable by a purely philosophical enquiry and only *clarified* and/or made more certain by divine revelation or the theological-doctrinal appropriation of that revelation.

Finnis, n. 33, at 29. So for Roman Catholics bishops pronouncing on controversial political issues, the non-establishment norm has no bite.

be committed and to which liberal democracy, as such, is committed. I have not argued in this postscript that every nation, or even every liberal democracy, should be committed to the non-establishment of religion. Whether it is a good thing (on balance) that government in the United States is constitutionally forbidden to establish religion, and whether it would be a good thing for government in, say, the United Kingdom to be forbidden to establish religion, are separate questions. An affirmative answer to the former question does not entail an affirmative answer to the latter (although an affirmative answer to the latter question may well be correct). It is often the case that, as Kent Greenawalt has written, "what principles of restraint, if any, are appropriate... depend on time and place, on a sense of the present makeup of a society, of its history, and of its likely evolution."[54]

It is an important question – but not one I address here – whether it would be a good thing for government in some, or even all, other liberal democracies to be forbidden to establish religion. As a citizen of the United States, my concern is whether it is a good thing that government in the United States is constitutionally forbidden to establish religion. As I said at the beginning of this postscript, there is, as far as I can tell, a virtual consensus among us citizens of the United

[54] Greenawalt, Private Consciences and Public Reasons, n. 2, at 130.

States, *including those of us who are religious believers*, that, all things considered, it is good both for religions and for social harmony that our lawmakers, state as well as federal, may not establish religion. The serious question among us, therefore, is not whether the constitutional law of the United States should include the non-establishment norm *but what the non-establishment norm should be understood to mean – to forbid – in one or another context*. In this postscript, I asked what the non-establishment norm, given its central meaning, should be understood to forbid in the context of lawmaking: Should it be understood to ban laws for which the only discernible rationale is religious? My answer: Yes, but only if the rationale depends on a religious premise that under the non-establishment norm government may not affirm.[55]

[55] Kent Greenawalt has articulated a position close to the one I defend here. See Greenawalt, "Religiously Based Judgments and Discourse in Political Life," n. 43, at 476–91:

> [A]s a matter of theoretical principle, I think enactment of a religious morality could violate the Establishment Clause, even if the religion, as a set lof beliefs and religious practices, is not promoted or endorsed in the more straighforward sense. . . . A law violates the Establishment Clause if the dominant ascertainable reason for its passage was a view that acts are immoral, based on a religious point of view and detached from any perspective about harm in this life that would be sufficient to justify a prohibition or regulation.

Id. at 487, 489. Moreover, Greenawalt says about his position what I have said in this postscript about mine: that his position "will rarely, if ever, lead a court to invalidate a law. . . . [T]he limits on appropriate grounds for laws [entailed by Greenawalt's position] are too narrow to have much practical significance." Id. at 489, 491.

Index

Index

Index

Index

Index

LaVergne, TN USA
19 January 2011
213008LV00002BA/14/P